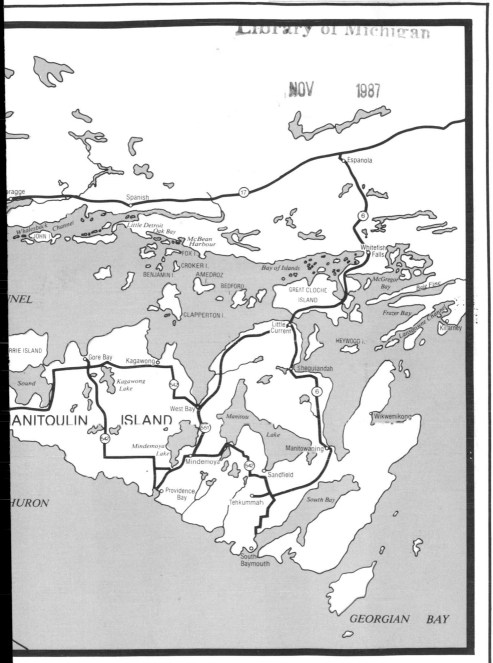

Third Edition

Well-Favored Passage

A Guide to Lake Huron's North Channel

Marjorie Cahn Brazer

HERON BOOKS

Manchester, Michigan

Copyright © 1975, 1982, 1987 by Marjorie Cahn Brazer
All rights reserved

Cover illustration "In The Benjamins," copyright © 1987 by Doug Hook

Photographs by the author

Endsheet maps prepared by Nanette Manhart

Published by Heron Books
536 Ann Arbor Hill
Manchester, Michigan 48158
Manufactured in The United States of America

Library of Congress Cataloging-in-Publication Data

Brazer, Marjorie Cahn.
  Well-favored passage.

  Includes index.
  1. North Channel Region (Huron, Lake, Mich. and Ont.)—
Description and travel—Guide-books. 2. Boats and
boating—North Channel (Huron, Lake, Mich. and Ont.)—
Guide-books. I. Title.
F1059.H95B7   1987   917.13'132044   87-8636
ISBN 0-942603-00-1

To Harvey
who shares with me the romance
of the North Channel

Contents

Charts

Preface To The Third Edition

In preparing a new edition of a guidebook the author must focus on the changes that have occurred since the last one. On the North Channel the most conspicuous changes in recent years have been wrought by pleasure boating. As the number of resident and visiting boats has multiplied, new marinas have been built and old ones enlarged, all with additional services. New yacht charterers have arrived. The Canadian Government has published new, improved charts, and replaced the old painted sticks and bull's eye beacons with new, modern buoyage. They have introduced continuous marine weather broadcasts, increased the number of radio correspondence channels, and expanded the network of safety and rescue services. Ashore, there are new shops and restaurants, formerly dirt roads are now paved, and new campgrounds have sprung up.

All of this is duly recorded in the present new edition of *Well-Favored Passage*. And, in keeping with the expansiveness of yachting life on the North Channel, a new chapter has been added, extending coverage to St. Joseph Channel, additional anchorages have been included, and new stories

Preface to the First Edition

To the mapmaker at a drawing board, the North Channel is a deep water passage between the Manitoulin Islands and the Ontario mainland at the northern extremity of Lake Huron; it connects St. Marys River on the west with Georgian Bay on the east. But to the mariner in a small boat it is far more than a place to be located by mathematically derived grids on a cold sheet of paper. To him it is a state of mind. It is a flight of the soul to a distant haunt—of peace, of timelessness, of mystery, of tempest, of aching beauty. Its very name evokes a mood, an ephemeral feeling—recall for those fortunate enough to have been there, yearning for those who have only heard tell.

To be sure, there are towns and villages, farms and mines along the North Channel, where the mundane business of the world proceeds at a suitable pace. But such places and activities are shorebound, confined. The North Channel is, above all, a free flowing world of water. Yet, where it meets the primitive land in a myriad of pristine forms and shapes, the earth and the water embrace to express together the real spirit of this beguiling corner of the world.

That reality is an intensely personal experience—to be discovered by each person who wanders there. A book such as this can offer only an introduction, a series of relatively impersonal geographical signposts. But those who seek beyond these printed words shall come to know, as did the Ottawa sages of old, why Gitchie Manitou, the benevolent spirit of the Master of Life, chose this place over all others for his home.

For the material contained in these pages the author is indebted to many sources: from the Jesuit fathers and *coureurs de bois* who first gazed westward over the blue waters of the Channel, to the fur traders who made it a highway to empire, to the lumber kings who built the towns as they demolished the forests, to the farmers and fishermen who came to settle, to the young Lieutenant Henry Wolsey Bayfield who first surveyed the waters of the Channel, to Commander J.G. Boulton and the Dominion Hydrographers who continued his work, to the friendly residents of today too numerous to name, and to the men and women of the Great Lakes Cruising Club, especially Howard C. Blossom, who have added as a labor of love an immeasurable understanding of the physiognomy and spirit of the North Channel. Special acknowledgement must go to Byron G. Turner, who gave the initial impetus to this project and support and encouragement throughout.

have been brought to light about the people and places on the Channel.

Yet, for all the changes the ineffable spirit of the North Channel prevails. The islands and the mountains, the rocks and the flowing water are timeless. In the towns and villages, where civilization takes hold, life proceeds in unhurried measure, adapting slowly and deliberately to the drumbeat of the world beyond. To return to Manitoulin Island and the villages of the north shore is to come home; the long ago is still there. The message in the preface to the first edition is still true.

~One ~

What to Know Before You Go

This is a book about a body of water, the shoreline that borders it, and the islands scattered through it. It is an introduction and guide to what the visitor may expect to find there, where he will find it, and how he can reach the places he seeks. Because the focus is marine, sailing directions and much of the information are oriented to the needs of the cruising yacht. But there are many visitors to the North Channel who come by car or bicycle, and who trailer or rent a boat for day cruising or boat camping. Indeed, the traveler who ventures no farther than the shoreline accessible by road has not actually met the North Channel. He must acquire, for however many hours or days he can spare, a sturdy vessel to carry him offshore to the islands or around to the mainland coves he will not find otherwise.

This introduction, then, is addressed to all comers—by land or by sea, in whatever kind of boat they choose to explore. Navigational information, generally expressed in terms of the draft limitations of larger cruising yachts, is valid also for the less restricted inboard or outboard runabout. Much of the material is directed specifically to the needs of the trailered boat (power or sail), the boat camper, and the motel or lodge guest who day cruises with or without fishing tackle. The distinction between *cruising yacht* and *small boat* for defining suitability of harbors is rather arbitrary. The first is defined to include boats propelled by inboard motors and/or with draft in excess of about two and one-half feet. Most sailboats would fall into this group. The small boat category, sometimes referred to as trailer boat or boat camping vessel, includes mostly outboard-powered motor boats of less than two and one-half foot draft and centerboard sailboats capable of reducing draft to that level. Boats in this group are as likely to be beached as anchored. Although the Indians and the voyageurs paddled for profit, the North Channel is not recommended for recreational canoeing, with a few exceptions which are noted.

In all cases, from the smallest outboard runabout to the largest cruiser or sailboat, it is assumed that the operator has a working knowledge of piloting, marine rules of the road, and the principles of safety in a boat. The skipper of a cruising boat must have (and the operator of a small boat would be wise to have) a compass, the latest marine charts of the area, and the knowledge of how to navigate with them. If he does not, he had best stay out of the North Channel. It is a place of profound beauty and inspiration, but it is a place fraught with anguish for the careless and the uninformed. On this assumption, sailing directions are presented only for harbors or channels not clearly delineated on the government charts. By no means is this book, or the chart portions reproduced in it, to be used as a navigational device. Rather, it is intended as a kind of nautical menu, offering sufficient description of the delectables available in the North Channel to enable the boating gourmet to make his choices for the day or season.

Anatomy of the North Channel

The North Channel is very young. The long travail of its birth from the continental ice sheet was taking place while the Emperor Hammurabi was codifying the ancient law of Babylon, when Menelaus later invaded Troy to regain his face and his queen and Moses led his people from Egypt proclaiming the Commandments of God, and later still when the venerable and sophisticated emperors of China were writing their laws on paper.

Yet this infant of the world's waterways is enfolded on its northern shores by the most ancient rocks of the planet—2.5 to 3 billion years old—formed even before Earth was protected by an atmosphere, let alone sustained life. The southern shores are much younger. They were created during a time when warm, salt seas lapped the feet of the austere Archean rocks to the north. During those eons the skeletal remains of billions of tiny marine organisms drifted slowly to the bottom, to build a great limestone reef that stretched in a 550-mile arc from present-day Niagara Falls, up the Bruce Peninsula, across the north side of Manitoulin Island and the Upper Peninsula of Michigan, to end in the Door Peninsula of Wisconsin. That was only about 400 million years ago, and for the last three thousand or so the North Channel has flowed between these disparate shores, marking their boundary, yet binding them together.

But the glaciers, whose meltwaters filled the North Channel as they retreated, had earlier scraped the land clean of topsoil in their advance to the southward. To this day, the basement rocks on either side of the Channel are clothed in the skimpiest of soil cover. Yet so remarkable are the forces of life that even this shallow soil supports a great variety of trees, grasses, shrubs, and flowers. Indeed, farming has been carried on on both sides of the Channel for over a hundred years, and on many of the offshore islands plants and trees seem to spring directly from the bare rock. It is possible to trace the evolution of plant life from the fossils of extinct algae in the limestone of Manitoulin, through the green and orange and black lichens clinging to wave-washed rocks on the islands, the moss in the crevices that weather and life have chiseled, the thin grasses, water hemlock, and junipers that sprout from tiny soil patches, blueberries spreading in the sheltered places, and, finally, oak, birch, and pine trees growing straight and lofty, where the soil layer thickens, until they create a great climax forest.

The original forest is gone—gone with the lumberjacks who cut it, the tugboat captains who towed the vast log rafts, and the sawmills that stripped resinous bark from the great pine boles and reduced them to boards for the houses of a continent. But it's been sixty years and more since they left, and the forest is slowly coming back. Perhaps this time around it will be harvested differently—for sustained yield in place of cut and run, and for the preservation of habitat for the other forms of life it sustains.

The North Channel has many nonhuman inhabitants. Its waters are well populated with bass, pike, walleye, perch, lake trout and muskellonge for the fortunate angler. There are also crayfish and freshwater clams for the taking. On the land are the usual creeping and crawling things—including occasional Massassauga rattlesnakes, dangerous to adults allergic to their venom and potentially lethal to children—chipmunks, squirrels, porcupines, deer, and black bear. Bridging both worlds are the frogs, performing nightly in the quiet anchorages which shoal to swamp, the water snakes, muskrat, otter, mink, and beaver. The last named is rarely seen but may often be heard in the quiet of the moonlight, diving with a resounding slap of his amazing tail. In the air the tiny biters are much in evidence, sharing the atmosphere with the more welcome songbirds and the winged swimmers—ducks, geese, loons, herons, gulls, and terns.

In short, where farms and villages have not intruded, the face of the North Channel looks much as it did 125 years ago when settlement first began. And the Ontario Government, under recent policies, intends to keep it that way. For decades Crown Land was considered something to be disposed of, especially to homesteaders. Serious agriculturists took up their claims early. More recent arrivals were city folk yearning for the peace and expansiveness of the wild north. They were happy to build a cabin or a palace, as taste and purse dictated, in return for the privilege of occupying a tract or an island of Crown Land on a 99-year lease, obtainable upon payment of a pittance to the government. No more. The thin soil of the North Channel can support only limited numbers of farms and the rocky lake bottom can absorb only so much sewage. Consequently North Channel Crown Lands are now closed to additional private leasing, although cottage building continues on private land. They have been designated as part of the North Georgian Bay Recreational Reserve, a special planning

district under jurisdiction of the Ministry of Natural Resources, that recognizes recreation as "the dominant . . .
highest priority use" in a fragile environment.

NORTH CHANNEL ROCK AND PINE, FRAZER BAY

Happily the Reserve includes most of the offshore islands of
the Channel and substantial stretches of mainland. Other large
mainland and Manitoulin Island tracts have long been designated Indian reserves. Unhappily for the Native North Americans, however, there is virtually no economic opportunity for
them on much of this reserve land, and it remains substantially
uninhabited. So between the lumber companies, the Ontario
Government, and the Ojibway and Ottawa Indians, most of the
North Channel remains wild and unpopulated—in effect a re-
verted wilderness—while summer cottages are clustered in a
few localities. Yet towns and villages are so artfully spaced
along both sides of its length as to afford the visitor essential
urban services no farther than thirty miles away from wherever he may be. They also provide an entertaining change of
pace as he moves in and out of the wilds.

Until the middle of the nineteenth century the North Channel
was little more than a lacustrine highway, a safe passageway
for frail birch bark canoes across the top of Lake Huron, pro-

tected by Gitchie Manitou's island from the sweep of those frightening seas. When the first white man arrived from Quebec, probably Governor Samuel de Champlain's scout, Étienne Brulé, about 1610, there were a few Indian villages. The Frenchmen who followed him, missionaries and fur traders, were eager to reach more important Indian settlements for the harvesting of souls and furs. They camped only briefly along the North Channel, although its 100 miles of sheltered waterway were indispensable to their business. During the eighteenth century huge brigades, laden with furs downbound and with supplies for the fur trade upbound, passed through the Channel en route between Montreal and Michilimackinac, the farthest reaches of the Great Lakes, and the great rivers of the West as far as the Rocky Mountains and the Arctic. Yet the first military post did not appear here until 1796 and the first white settlers did not take up residence until 1820.

Even after that, farming and village settlement proceeded slowly until the great lumbering boom of the late nineteenth century. Many of the towns along the Channel date their origins from that. But by the 1920s the virgin timber was mostly logged out. Fishing was important for a few decades until overfishing and invasion of the lamprey eel all but destroyed the fishery in the 1950s. By then tourism was beginning to be taken seriously, and it has been growing ever since, both by land and by water. In recent years some commercial fishing has returned, with suppression of the lamprey and resurgence of lake trout and whitefish. There is still pulpwood lumbering, and a few wood processing plants and mining operations lend a mild touch of industry. But for the most part the North Channel remains a quiet corner of the world, where the pace of life is sedate, and old-fashioned neighborliness defines the social scene. The visitor who seeks peace and beauty finds them. Still a relatively safe place for small boats, the North Channel is no longer just a "passage through," but a cherished destination for its own sake.

Logistics of a North Channel Adventure

Although the North Channel lies within a day's drive (less than 500 miles) of some twenty million people, its shores are remote, accessible only by two automobile routes. Trans-Canada Highway 17 runs along the north shore, connecting Sault Ste. Marie on the west with Sudbury on the east. Visitors from eastern Ontario and Quebec or Michigan, Illinois, and points west approach by this road. From Ohio, Pennsylvania, New York, and as an alternative for residents of southern Michigan and Ontario, there is another route of access via Ontario Highway 6 up the Bruce Peninsula, thence by ferry from Tobermory to Manitoulin Island. Both drives are scenic; the southern approach is somewhat more pastoral. Although Highway 17 is the trans-Canada route it is still two-lane in this area and heavily traveled, while Route 6, for all its lesser importance, is not an inferior road and carries far less truck traffic. Its major disadvantage is the necessity of meeting a ferry schedule.

The two roads meet at Espanola, where panoramic Highway 6 runs south from Route 17 for 53 kilometers (32 miles) to cross the North Channel at Little Current and connect with the ferry at South Baymouth 64 kilometers (38 miles) away. Where you live and the location of your chosen headquarters for cruising the Channel will determine which approach route you select. For a more inclusive trip you might want to come one way and return the other. Visitors coming all the way by boat also face two choices of approach; these are described in Chapters Two and Six. There are launch ramps for trailered boats in every village and at most marinas, also identified in succeeding chapters. Many are dirt-based; some are concrete.

Logistics become a bit more complicated when a cruising boat must pick up and discharge guests who join the crew on the North Channel. For boat guests coming by car there are several choices of rendezvous on both sides of the Channel, discussed, in turn, in succeeding chapters. Again the decision is a matter of who is coming from where. Bear in mind that unless there are departing guests who will drive the car home it is necessary to return to the same port.

For boat guests who arrive by public transportation, pickup is feasible at several places. Greyhound buses run six times a day each way between Sudbury and Sault Ste. Marie on Highway 17. With air terminals in both of those cities, it's not difficult to make connections to and from the outside world at Bruce Mines, Thessalon, Blind River, and Spragge on the north shore. A.J. Bus Lines from Little Current meets the morning Greyhounds at the Arena Grill in Española for connections to Manitoulin. They also serve the island on a rather complicated schedule between Wikwemikong, Manitowaning, Little Current, and Gore Bay. Killarney, at the extreme eastern end of the Channel, also runs a local van (the mail bus) into downtown Sudbury every morning and back in the afternoon, except Sunday, which connects with the airport limousine. Call Manitoulin Transport to reserve space.

There is one more mode of access, suitable both for resort-based tourists and visitors to a cruising yacht. That is by air. There is no scheduled airline service to the North Channel itself (Sault Ste. Marie and Sudbury lie beyond), but there is a general airport at Gore Bay on Manitoulin Island, a landing strip near Thessalon on the north shore, and an airfield at Killarney, that can accommodate private planes and charter flights. Lauzon Aviation of Algoma Mills on the north shore and Ramsey Airline in Sudbury provide charter float plane service. For a price, passengers can be picked up in their home location and flown up to the North Channel or returned therefrom. These companies also offer charter flights for camping among the maze of lakes deep in the interior of northern Ontario.

So much for how to find your way to the North Channel. What should you bring with you? It's not complicated. Dress is informal throughout. A man might want to carry a jacket and tie and a woman might bring a not-too-sheer summer dress for an occasional change of sartorial pace. But slacks with sport shirt or blouse, as the case may be, are entirely acceptable in every dining room. Otherwise, the usual northen summer play clothes are in order—minimal for hot days, with headgear and dark glasses for protection from the sun, sweater and windbreaker for in-between and cloudy weather, and warm jacket, slacks, and socks for nights that can be really nippy. Ear muffs and mittens are not essential, but it does rain on the North Channel; be prepared with storm suit or waterproof raincoat.

Laundromats are well enough spaced that you don't need to load up numerous changes of clothing. Two to four is sufficient, depending upon space and how often you're willing to do the washing. Warm bedding is also important; night temperatures can drop into the thirties. Boat shoes with the hard-gripping treads designed not to leave scuff marks are adequate for most hiking expeditions ashore. But if any serious cross-country walking is to be done, sturdy, waterproof hiking boots are in order.

In all the towns along the North Channel you can buy necessary personal items that may have been forgotten, although you may not always find your favorite brand. But not all of these places have pharmacies, so you should bring any regularly used prescription drugs in sufficient supply for the duration of the visit. Include an antihistamine, prescribed by your own physician, for dealing with a possible allergic response to an insect bite or poison ivy while you're out in the wilds. Nor are there any opticians on the Channel; bring an extra pair of glasses. Every traveler should, of course, carry a basic first-aid kit, but for boating in isolated areas it's essential. You can't pack it into a kit, but the members of your party should carry knowledge of cardio-pulmonary resuscitation techniques, and nonswimmers should at least be "drown-proofed." There are physicians and dentists in most of the towns and hospitals in three of them, should skilled, professional attention be needed.

Edibles are obtainable on an as-you-go basis along the North Channel, but their degree of sophistication varies greatly from place to place. You should plan to bring your *pâté aux truffles* and eels marinated in wine sauce from home, while basic canned and packaged foods are available almost everywhere. Packaged cold cuts can usually be found, but the quality and quantity of fresh meat may be superior in one place while practically nil in another. Fresh fish is rarely sold in food stores. Aside from your own catch, you must find a commercial fishing boat or the fish market in Killarney. As for fresh produce, the local harvest comes in late, but many of the stores stock imported summer fruits and vegetables. Solid and stolid potatoes, cabbages, lettuce, carrots, onions, and apples are found everywhere; tomatoes, squash, peaches, melon, cucumbers, and celery in most; artichokes and pineapples in none. Then there are the comestibles that are especially good along the North

Channel: dairy products, Peak Frean cookies, and Canadian pea meal bacon.

Liquor and beer are sold in Ontario only in government outlets, usually separate ones for the two forms of intoxicant. The towns where these facilities are located will be identified in succeeding chapters. The beer and whiskey selections are typically excellent, and the choice of wines is improving. In addition to Ontario products, some nonvintage European wines are available. Depots for returning deposit cans and bottles are not located logically in the stores, but are usually out on the highway somewhere, inaccessible to boaters.

All of the larger towns on the North Channel have hardware stores, and most of them carry an astonishing array of items, including camping gear. But here again, brands are limited, so it is advisable to bring your basic equipment with you. Fishing gear is the most extensively stocked item, and lures and bait can be purchased in almost every establishment that sells anything at all. The availability of marine hardware is another story. Bring from home as much in the way of spare parts as you can predict the need for and stow. There are a couple of small marine stores, but they and the local boat yards are stocked with only minimal and more or less universally used items for cruising boats. If you find yourself in need of something important, like a propeller or a winch handle, you may have to wait days for it to be shipped from Toronto or farther. For outboard motors, however, there are more numerous repair shops with most standard parts available. There are a few places where a cruising boat can be hauled out on a railway or travelift. They are identified in subsequent chapters.

Marine charts are sold at several places along the Channel but, with one exception noted later, not every chart that is needed may be in stock at each place. It's wise to buy the charts you plan to use by mail order from the Canadian Hydrographic Service before you leave home. Other publications that should also be obtained from the same source are *Sailing Directions, Great Lakes, Volume II; Inland Waters List of Lights, Buoys and Fog Signals;* and *Radio Aids to Navigation.* (See Appendix C for a complete list and ordering information.)

Notes to Americans: Before you leave the United States in a pleasure boat that exceeds 30 feet you must pay a $25 annual fee to United States Customs, for which you will receive a receipt and decal to place on your boat. This transaction can be handled by mail if you send for form 339 from your nearest Customs office or write to U.S. Customs Service, P.O. Box 198151, Atlanta, Georgia 30384. What you must obtain in person, however, is a Canadian Border Landing Card, Form I-68. This is issued by the United States Immigration and Naturalization Service under special regulations for the Great Lakes Waterways. It, too, is a season pass, issued free of charge when you present proof of citizenship or resident alien status (birth certificate or naturalization paper, not a driver's license) to an immigration officer at a U.S. Port of Entry. This program also applies only to people on boats over 30 feet, and one form can list the entire crew, or individual forms can be issued. It is possible to leave the country without these two documents, but you may have serious trouble getting back in when you apply for re-entry. If you have been shopping in Canada and have goods to declare you must also report to U.S. Customs on return.

On entering Canada you are required to report to Canadian Customs and Immigration at the first port you reach in Canadian waters. (Car travelers are stopped at border crossing points on the highways.) The telephone number for Canada Customs is usually posted at a public telephone on the dock. Sometimes you will complete the formalities by phone; on other occasions an officer may come to see you at dockside. In either case you need neither passport nor visa, although you should be able to present valid identification. Your dog needs a vaccination certificate signed by a licensed veterinarian. Your boat will be registered by an assigned number, and can remain in Canada up to twelve months. There are a few items not allowed into the country, such as certain kinds of plants, and revolvers, pistols, or fully automatic firearms. You are required to limit your food supply to two days' consumption for your party, and the alcoholic beverage allowance is forty ounces per person. Ontario requires that every marine toilet be equipped with a holding tank.

Although the stores all accept American dollars, they are not likely to give as favorable an exchange as the banks do because of the uncertainties of fluctuating rates and the collection costs they face. So it's a good idea to buy your Canadian cash at a bank before you leave home or in the towns en route, to get the latest, big money market exchange rate. Credit card purchases will reflect the exchange rate at the time your account is debited. ·

Canada joined the rest of the world in "going metric" several years ago. Road mileages are posted in kilometers; temperatures are reported in centigrade (celsius); more and more charts show depths and heights in meters; and foods are packaged and priced by the liter and the kilogram. A pocket conversion table is a handy thing to carry.

Particularities of North Channel Navigation

Because the Channel is protected from the long fetch of Lake Huron seas, don't be misled into believing it tame. One hundred miles long, up to twenty miles wide, and from 0 to 250 feet deep, the North Channel is large enough to offer sea room and challenge to any rag sailor, a bouncy ride to the heaviest power boat, and a few wind-whipped seas and tempests of its own. Storms come up as suddenly here as anywhere on the Great Lakes. But the supreme virtue of the North Channel is that there are enough sheltered stretches to permit boating in small craft on many a day that would keep one harbor-bound on the open lake. Furthermore, the distances between one alluring harbor and another are relatively short, so that if one is caught out in weather, shelter is never very far away.

Nevertheless, mariners, here as everywhere, are governed by weather and sea conditions. In summer, both tend to be relatively mild on the North Channel. Long, sunny days are warm to hot, cooling off at night to sweater and sleeping comfort. Winds, prevailing from south and southwest through west, tend to be light, especially where their fetch is broken up by islands and land masses, to the occasional consternation of sailors. The usual daily pattern sees the wind freshen mid-morning, perhaps lull around noon, peak in late afternoon, and die out in an early evening calm. Although protected waters are usually quiet, the open waters of the

Channel can develop quite a chop, and may build seas as high as four to six feet in strong winds.

Fog is relatively rare, and when it does occur it usually burns off by late morning. But there is a different visibility problem peculiar to these waters—summer haze. This atmospheric phenomenon drapes the North Channel in soothing tones of blue, shading to mauve, but the aesthetic effect can be less than welcome when one is trying to judge distances or locate a distant navigational aid. The problem is rarely severe, but it does exist.

Summer is defined by most visitors as the more dependable months of July and August, but June brings many a rare day, even if the nights are a little chillier, and September offers sharper light for nature's paintbrush and the warmest water temperatures for swimming, along with more frequent rain. For anglers late spring and early fall are the best times.

As on all the Great Lakes, water levels are critical to the safe enjoyment of harbors and shallow passages. Most of the North Channel is very deep; its configuration below the surface reflects its imposing elevations above. But some of the north side harbors and islands rest on shallow banks, where channels must be dredged through to port facilities, and anchorages are accessible only to shallow draft vessels.

Great lakes water levels fluctuate from year to year in an irregular cyclical pattern, and within each year from one season to the next. They are usually highest in late spring and early summer, when the lakes are fed by melting snows and spring rains, and drop to their lowest seasonal level during the early winter. In 1985 and 1986 record high water levels were attained throughout the system, posing severe problems of shoreline erosion and damage to marina docks and facilities. Extreme low water, on the other hand, such as we had during the early 1960s, can strand shoreside developments high and dry. Either case poses hazards in shoal passages and wilderness anchorages. When the water is excessively high rocks that are ordinarily exposed lurk invisibly just beneath the surface, and when the lake levels are excessively low rocks and islets appear confusingly on the seascape that are not shown on the chart. All mariners can do is remain constantly aware of how the lakes stand at the moment in relation to the mean low water depths recorded on their charts.

The continuous marine weather broadcasts of Canadian Coast Guard Radio include the latest weekly mean water levels. In the North Channel area these are issued from VBB Sault Ste. Marie through Silver Water on channel 83B and from VBC Wiarton through Killarney on channel 21B. Weather is broadcast in both the MAFOR (MArine FORecast) code and English language, and includes near shore forecasts for small craft on the specific waters of the North Channel. Notices to shipping about malfunctioning navigational aids and other unexpected hazards are broadcast at the same time.

Whether you ply the waters of the North Channel in a ten-foot rowboat or a sixty-foot three-masted schooner, there are a few navigational techniques that are special to this body of water. First, boats rarely move after dark. Although the port towns are marked by at least one navigation light, they are of limited visibility and often difficult to distinguish from other shore lights. Lighted buoys to mark hazards in open water are infrequent. And certainly no wilderness anchorage, by definition unlit, can be sensibly approached at night. With daylight saving time, seventeen hours of sunlit cruising should be enough for any boat to reach its destination before nightfall.

Even when the sun is shining there are a few tricks. Cruise eastward after noon, if you can, and cruise westward in the morning, especially if you are approaching an anchorage. Where the waters are shallow and there are no buoys or beacons to identify the shoals, it's essential for visibility to have the sun at its zenith or behind you. For this kind of eyeball navigation there is nothing more comforting than a pair of polaroid sunglasses. They cut miraculously through the glare and penetrate even dark waters to show you the boulders and pinnacles waiting for you off course below. All boats, but especially those of deep draft, should post a polaroid-sunglasses-fitted lookout on the bow as the skipper proceeds dead slow into an anchorage or through some of the hairier island passages.

As you may have concluded, there is not a lot of buoyage on the North Channel. What is there is directed to and from

Sault Ste. Marie. That is, reds are on the right going westward or to the Sault and on the left moving eastward away from that city. But instead of the nuns and cans common to the ocean seacoasts and inland waters below, the North Channel sports mostly spars, painted green, red, or striped, in the conventional buoyage patterns. From a distance, especially if the sun is in your eyes, the color of these spars may be hard to identify. Their shape is intended to be a guide, as the reds have pointed tops and the greens are flat. But that doesn't always help because many of the North Channel's spars are uncomfortably small.

KILLARNEY EAST LIGHT

   To supplement the spar buoys some of the rocky offshore islands are marked with beacons. These are mainly steel posts, topped by either a square with a black bull's eye or a triangle with a red one. In a few places you'll find an older version—three-sided, triangular, slatted structures, perched like little dunce caps on the rock and painted bright red or orange. Beacons tend to be more visible than spar buoys. In fact, some are so conspicuous, if the sun is right, as to seem closer than they actually are. On some of the prominent headlands the characteristic Canadian lighthouse stands, a four-sided white wood structure with a red topknot. In a few passages there are ranges; some are lit and some are unlighted daybeacons. These are the best aids of all; one only wishes there were more of them.

Given the sparseness and poor visibility of North Channel buoyage, especially among the islands and bays of the north shore, navigation becomes much more of a personal affair. Let the eyes of the pilot be sharp. Often the only way to know for certain where you are is to keep a finger on the chart and a strictly accurate count of all the islands as you pass them. This takes a bit of practice, as many of the gigantic boulders sporting a plumage of pine look alarmingly identical. Large cruising boats should keep the depth sounder going on the approach to an anchorage or a narrow passage, and even a small outboard boat can benefit from a portable depth finder to ease gunkholing.

If you haven't guessed already, all of this adds up to one word in island- and narrow passage-making—slow. You can hoist full sail or open up the throttles in large areas of open water in the North Channel, but in cruising the tight places and approaching anchorages, dead slow under power enables you to reverse your field quickly if a rock or shoal suddenly appears where you don't expect it. Not all of them are charted by any means. Is it necessary to add that a boat should *always* enter a harbor where there are other boats, whether urban or wilderness, at dead slow? You may even do yourself a favor—it's so much easier to dock or anchor when you aren't wallowing in your own wake.

Despite all precautions, circumstances do arise in which a boat or its crew needs help. Canadian Coast Guard rescue operations are handled through the Rescue Coordination Centre at Trenton on Lake Ontario. A distress call on channel 16 to the nearest VHF radio station (VBB Sault Ste. Marie or VBC Wiarton) will be relayed to Trenton, where appropriate action is taken through the Coast Guard base at Goderich or Meaford if a cutter or air evacuation is needed. More likely, a North Channel emergency will be handled either through the crash boat at Tobermory (a small version of the cutter) or the seasonal mobile rescue unit at Bruce Mines, depending upon where the distressed boat is located. The mobile unit is a high-powered inflatable, staffed by specially trained college students, who are capable of giving medical first aid and CPR, as well as doing simple boat repairs and towing craft under thirty feet. Government assistance is supplemented by the highly effective Canadian Marine Rescue Auxiliary. This is a voluntary association of private boat owners (yachtsmen and commercial fishermen) under contract to the Ministry of Transport to serve in assigned areas on 24-hour call. In the North Channel area they are located in St. Marys River, Meldrum Bay, Gore Bay, Kagawong, Little Current, and Killarney. If a boat is overdue, land-based family or friends should call the Trenton Rescue Coordination Centre at 1-800-267-7270.

While the primary purpose for which Canadian Coast Guard Radio was established is the safety function, it also provides public correspondence telephone service. Ship-to-shore calls can be placed and received through VBB Sault Ste. Marie from a boat west of Little Current, and through VBC Wiarton east of that point. Both stations have extended facility ranges, commonly known as relay or slave stations, located at Silver Water and Killarney, respectively. Because of the congestion problem on channel 16, call for telephone service directly on their working channels, 24, 26 and 85 for Wiarton, 26, 27 and 88 for Sault Ste. Marie. Marinas are permitted to monitor only channel 68, so if you want to make an advance reservation you must call on that frequency in order to reach them at all.

The first marine survey of the North Channel was conducted by a talented young officer of the British Navy, Lieutenant Henry Wolsey Bayfield, in 1822. Seventy years later Commander J.G. Boulton updated the measurements. These two officers conferred most of the names on the islands, rocks, points and shoals, and in some cases they dug pretty deeply to come up with one. Most of the persons they honored are long forgotten, but those who can still be traced will be recalled for a brief moment in the chapters that follow.

The newest survey, using a sophisticated technology Bayfield and Boulton could never have dreamed of, began about ten years ago and is almost complete. As a consequence the whole charting scheme for the Channel is undergoing revision. Several of the new charts have been issued and more will be forthcoming within the next five years. (See Appendix C for the current list.) There is not likely to be one chart of the entire North Channel, as defined in this book, but the scales and coverage will vary from 1:60,000 over a broad segment, to 1:25,000 for detail. One very large scale folio chart for small craft was issued several years ago, and more of those may be forthcoming as well. For a while it may be confusing to move back and forth between current chart editions, which show heights and depths in feet and distances in statute miles, and the newest charts, which use metric measurements, so you must stay alert to these differences and keep your conversion table handy.

To complicate matters a bit further, one antiquated chart remains in effect for a small segment of the North Channel. 2286 is printed in black and white, with shoal areas tinged in blue, and records soundings in fathoms in a hard-to-read script. Furthermore, the soundings refer to an obsolete chart datum, so you must subtract 4.7 feet from the readings to make them comparable with the current plane of reference. But 2286 has one feature that has regrettably been deleted from the new-style charts. Display of the contours of bluffs and mountains as shaded fringes, rather than faint contour lines, is not only far more artistic, but enables the reader to get a quick impression of the lay of the land, very helpful when counting islands and where aids to navigation are scarce. When 2286 is finally retired you should fold it away carefully with Great-Grandmother's bustle. It still bears some of the graphics penned over 160 years ago by Lieutenant Bayfield and may become a valuable collector's item.

Harbor Life

In the old days, when steamships and ferries called at all the North Channel ports, each was fronted by a government wharf These were usually built of concrete, with a sloping cement ramp leading to the ship's hold. A white painted shed with green trim stood at the back of the dock for storage of freight while it awaited loading, with a smaller room at one end where passengers bought their tickets from a wicketed window and sat on benches until their ship came in.

The old days ended not so long ago. The last ferry, for decades the lifeline of the North Channel, made its last run in 1968. But when you arrive at most of these towns you will still see the concrete wharf studded with ship's bollards. Now it sprouts broad, planked wings (sometimes freshly creosoted to the consternation of boatkeepers), edged with wood tie-up rails or small metal rings or cleats more suitable to small craft. The old shed buildings still stand, too, although some of them may be almost unrecognizable under their transformations into restaurants and marine service shops. Either the old building or the end of the newer dock will display a daymark and light.

When you pull up to a government wharf for fuel or an overnight stay you will dock alongside, end to end with other boats. But often there is a basin behind the wharf with floating slips for overnight dockage. In either case you will want fenders, hung at the water line at docks awash in high water or on floats. Most government docks are operated by the municipality in which they are located; on some a private concessionaire runs the services and collects the modest public fee for dockage. There are also several new public and private marinas along the North Channel; each will be described in subsequent chapters. Most government docks and all marinas provide electric power, but some of the connections are two-wire 15-amp plugs, some supply 20 amps, and some are three-wire 30-amp installations. Some marinas furnish adapters if your cable end doesn't fit; others do not. It's hard to say, however, just which type of adapter you should bring with you to meet all circumstances.

There are no special techniques for anchoring in the North Channel that are different from good practice anywhere. Come in dead slow with the sun behind you, if possible, watch your depths, and drop the hook far enough from shore to allow the boat to swing 360 degrees on a scope of at least five to one. Most Channel anchorages have good holding in mud. If you have trouble with a dragging anchor you may have set down on a pile of old logs and/or sawdust; try another spot nearby.

Many people like to tie off to trees on shore in those anchorages where the shoreline rock faces drop straight down. If you don't have a sufficiently nimble crew to leap ashore with lines in hand, you can carry them by dinghy and bring the boat gently up to the rock face. A small outboard boat, with motor lifted, can usually be worked into a tiny "bay" between projecting rock slopes for safe lying and easy hopping to a campsite on shore.

A great many of the anchorages in the North Channel are uninhabited, and I make the assumption that for others, as well as for me, these are the best kind. We come here in the first place in order to reap the benefits of wilderness. I assume, as well, that solitary cottagers, in the few places they are found, also like it that way. In short, if you can avoid anchoring near a cottage, do so—for the inhabitants' sake and for yours, although in some of the cottage-studded bays that isn't always possible. In those places boaters are more likely to suffer at the hands of cottagers, who race around in their speedboats, oblivious to the consternation caused by their wakes on an anchored boat. Nevertheless, at the risk of offending my readers, I must remind them to be scrupulous about observing the usual courtesies—no wake from either an inboard or outboard boat; no loud voices or radios in the evenings, when every sound is greatly magnified over water; no beaching of dinghies on the cottagers' shoreline; and, of course, no dumping of anything in the water. This list, I might add, applies with equal force when sharing an unpopulated anchorage with another boat or boats. Furthermore, if you must run a generator in an anchorage try to avoid doing so at sundown when the birdsong is sweetest, or after dark when neighbors may be trying to sleep. One last word on wilderness courtesy: trash is a growing menace. Leave none behind you. In fact, try to take away more than you bring; pack out somebody else's beer cans along with your own.

Which brings us to camping. Strictly speaking, the general public is entitled to visiting rights only on public land. But since Crown Land is indistinguishable from uninhabited Indian reserve or private property, custom allows anyone to go ashore where the land is not clearly in active private use. And in this broad category the North Channel offers some ideal camping sites—open, flat rock for tenting away from the woodsy bugs and for building fires away from the woodsy combustibles, yet with sufficient forest in the background to afford a supply of fuel for the campfire, burial sites for human waste, and the murmur of pines as you fall asleep. These same rocks provide safe, miniature "harbors" at which to tie up your small boat.

Whether you're living ashore in your tent or merely having a cookout ashore from your live-aboard boat, remember that fire is the single greatest threat to your beneficent surroundings. Build your campfire on a slab of bare rock and contain it within a circle of small rocks. Use only the dead wood you find lying about; there is no need to hack at trees on the North Channel. When you are ready to leave your fire, douse and stir it many times, then scatter the ashes and the ring of rocks to leave no trace of your presence. If you use your paper trash for kindling, make sure it is all combustible. If a bit of tinfoil or a bottle cap is inadvertently included, fish it out of the dead fire to wrap in a plastic bag with your garbage, bottles, and cans, to be taken to the next dock with a public trash container.

The low rocks at the water's edge are good for another purpose besides campsites. The chilly waters of lake Huron are warmest in the shallows close to shore, and the great slabs of granite that underpin the Channel make ideal swimming platforms. Do *not*, under any circumstances, dive from these. Almost everywhere the bottom is so uneven as to present hazardous peaks thrusting upward to strike an unwary cranium. Rather, step or slide off the warm rock into the cool water, and when you've done your splashing and swimming slither back over the sloping, slippery stones to bask contentedly on the hot surface. And don't count on finding your favorite swimming platform from year to year; the rocks have a habit of appearing and disappearing with changes in water level.

While I would prefer to rhapsodize exclusively on the beauties and enjoyments of the North Channel, I would be misleading in the extreme were I to omit mention of buzzing, biting insects—in particular, mosquitoes. A skipper of my acquaintance theorizes that there is a given population of mosquitoes in any anchorage, and that it divides itself among however so many boats are moored there. If you are fortunate enough to enjoy solitude in a wilderness hideaway you will receive the undivided attention of the entire mosquito population. They emerge in hordes with the dropping of the sun to the horizon. The only solution is to observe the sunset from screened cabin or tent, light a mosquito coil before sunset to get a head start, go to bed at nightfall (often they hover until daybreak), and outlast the pesky things until morning. Only if it's very windy can you really enjoy a night under the stars in July and early August; by mid-August their heyday is thankfully past. Deerflies and blackflies also present a menace. Although they are less numerous than mosquitoes, they do their dirty work by day and are less easily outwitted.

How the Rest of This Book is Organized

Having disposed of all the general practicalities in chapter one—how to get to the North Channel, what to bring, the weather and sea conditions you'll find, how to navigate, dock, and anchor, camping courtesies, bug warfare, etc.—succeeding chapters will get to the things you really want to hear about, like where to go and what there is to see and do when you get there. There is no "ideal" cruise plan presented. What is ideal is a matter of individual taste. The gregarious will enjoy best a cruise that takes them from town to resort to town, where there is much socializing on the docks. Those who seek solitude will not find themselves alone in every anchorage, especially between July 4 and August 15. But they will plan a voyage to keep them longest among the isolated bays and offshore anchorages, which they might have to themselves often enough to satisfy their minimum desire. For almost everyone there is something captivating along the North Channel, except opulent luxury. Where a visit might take you depends, as well, on the amount of time you have. There are those who "do it" in less than a week; for others it requires a lifetime.

In the chapters to follow each place—town, passage, anchorage—will first be described in terms of what's interesting about it. Its life story might be told, followed by sailing directions for reaching it and, in the case of towns, facilities, services, and entertainments to be found there. Chart segments are reproduced for those anchorages where the approach and entrance are not entirely clear without a diagram, and where sailing courses are explained in the text. All courses are given as true. Water depths reported always refer to low water chart datum.

The wintertime armchair traveler can read through the descriptions and anecdotes, skipping over the how-to-do-it sections, usually labeled "Approach" and "Dockage and Marine Services," until he needs them. Trailer and rental boat-launching bases and charterers are identified, but only American or European plan hotels, motels, and resorts are discussed. Space does not permit identification of the scores of housekeeping cottage resorts and campgrounds in the area; published listings for those are noted in Appendix D. Virtually every resort has boats and motors for rent. By and large prices at marinas, restaurants, motels, and resorts are modest, compared with other cruising and touring areas. As expected, the more elaborate resorts, offering more sophisticated amenities, charge higher rates than average for the region.

In all cases judgement is passed—you get my opinion as to the merits of this town or that anchorage. Unless otherwise specified, you can assume that all anchorages have at least one good campsite, though not all anchorages are included in this book. One of the deep satisfactions of cruising is the joy of discovery. Rather than deprive you, I leave some hideaways unmentioned. These are yours to find and to claim as your own.

The book is arranged in elliptical geographic sequence, west to east along the north shore, then east to west along the south side. Keep in mind that the Channel is only about twenty miles wide at its widest point, and much narrower than that in most places. It's easy to cross back and forth and a zig-zag cruise may, in fact, be the best plan for catching the wind, food shopping, and similar important considerations. Literary, not navigational, convenience has dictated the perimeter plan of the book. Now it's time to embark.

~Two ~

Western Entrance and St. Joseph Channel

The North Channel is open ended; entrance can be made from the east or from the west. Cruising boats from Ohio, southeast Michigan, southwest Ontario, and points east are offered a choice. According to which Lake Huron shore they hug on the northward voyage, they can come around either end of Manitoulin Island. Those who head on the Channel from Lake Michigan or Lake Superior ports will enter from the west. The trailered boat has many choices, from both ends and the middle, each to be described in its appropriate place.

Precisely where the North Channel begins on the west is a matter of some ambiguity. The International Boundary Commission, working between 1818 and 1828, designated Drummond and St. Joseph Islands as inhabitants of St. Marys River. North and/or eastward of these two lay the North Channel. Yet St. Joseph Channel, running northward of that island, is distinctly North Channel country scenically and geologically and bears little resemblance to the rest of St. Marys River. It is small in area, fifteen miles by two and one-half at it's widest. The south shore is undulating and pastoral, while the north side is scribed with the bold rock and deep green pines that is the North Channel's signature. If the height of your mast does not exceed 38 feet, you can meander the entire fifteen miles, sampling the two villages and six anchorages. If you are taller you must turn around at the fixed highway bridge, and pass up one of the villages.

To reach the North Channel from open Lake Huron you follow the ship channel through De Tour Passage into St. Marys River. At Pipe Island Twins Light you may leave the pathway of the long, gliding lake freighters by shaping your course northward to the flashing red off Pirate Island and following the international boundary along St. Joseph's shore. Or you can turn eastward into the maze of bun-shaped green islands of Potagannising Bay. Here, if the day is too far gone to proceed, there is a choice of dockage or anchorage.

Along the latter course it's about seven miles from Pipe Island Twins to Drummond Island village, where Drummond Island Yacht Haven offers alongside tieup for visiting boats in 10 feet, gasoline, diesel fuel, fresh water, electric power, ice, showers, laundromat, repair services, and a marine store. Proprietor Denny Bailey is a U.S. Customs Agent, who can check in returning U.S. boats or entering Canadians. A long shoal makes out into the bay just east of the marina entrance, and the small private buoys that mark it are not readily visible to a newcomer; keep a sharp lookout.

A similar seven miles from Pipe Island Twins Light is the peaceful, land-locked anchorage at Harbor Island. A cottage or two remain near the entrance, but the island is owned by the Nature Conservancy, to be preserved forever wild. Whichever stopover you elect, you'll be rehearsing for your North Channel cruise as you thread the look-alike islands to reach them. Start counting.

Milford Haven
Charts 2251 and U.S. 14882

If you follow the St. Joseph Island shore from Pipe Island Twins Light a run of nine miles brings you to the tranquil anchorage of Milford Haven. St. Joseph Island, 28 miles long by 15 miles wide, was bypassed by white missionaries and traders until the British Government built a military post there in 1796 after the Jay Treaty forced them to give up Mackinac Island. Once the garrison was ensconced, a trading village grew up around the fort. The opening shot of the War of 1812 on the Great Lakes was fired by the commander of Fort St. Joseph when he sallied forth on July 13, 1812 to retake Fort Mackinac from the Americans. The British remained in that stronghold until the 1814 Treaty of Ghent restored it to the United States. Now they faced a dilemma.

The international boundary was stipulated by treaty to run through the middle of the Great Lakes and their connecting waterways, but these waters had not yet been surveyed to determine just where the middle lay. British military authorities reckoned that when the St. Marys River line was finally drawn St. Joseph Island would go to the Americans, while Britain would get Drummond Island. They guessed wrong. Abandoning St. Joseph Island in 1815 to build a new base on Drummond, where the traders followed them, they were ultimately obliged to give that one up, too, in 1828. Instead of returning to Fort St. Joseph, which they had cannibalized for the Drummond Island buildings, they moved a couple of hundred miles away to Penetanguishene on Georgian Bay. St. Joseph Island remained virtually uninhabited for almost another quarter century before it began to evolve into the farming and quiet summer resort community it is today.

Throughout its history America, the land of opportunity, has attracted an assortment of upper-class eccentrics along with the poor and the persecuted. Canada early became a haven for British younger sons and military officers seeking either a genteel life on a slim property income, or frontier adventure to dissipate the ennui of Europe at peace. Major William Kingdon Rains had a less conventional motive—too many wives.

Rains started out respectably enough. He was born into a gentle Welsh family in 1789, educated at the Royal Military

Academy, and commissioned a second lieutenant in 1805, at the age of sixteen. After twelve years of service under the Duke of Wellington he retired at a captain's half pay to study engineering, get married, and father several offspring. Unhappy in the marriage, Rains escaped to another three years of active duty at Malta, with promotion to the rank of major.

1828 found him back in England, restless, unloved and middle-aged. Unable to alter the last condition, he took care of the second by obtaining legal separation from his wife. He then set up a happy home with seventeen-year-old Frances Doubleday, the refined and educated daughter of a Welsh attorney. Rains had retained custody of his younger son, and Frances soon presented him with another. In 1830, with love now secure in his life, he decided to assuage his restlessness by selling his commission and emigrating to Canada. But Frances had only one living relative, and the prospect of being separated, probably forever, from her beloved sister, Eliza, was more than she could bear. William didn't hesitate; Eliza would go with them to the new life.

When they first settled on Lake Simcoe there was little cause for raised eyebrows; the refined couple's history and illegitimate status had been left behind. Rains' ability, education and experience were recognized in his appointment as Commissioner of Peace. But by 1834 he was getting restless again. With two associates he petitioned for a land grant on frontier St. Joseph Island, where only a few French and Indians were currently living. Furthermore, his domestic affairs had come to need the obscurity that such a remote location offered.

In 1835 the Rains family and partners set sail with a few settlers from Penetanguishene at the foot of Georgian Bay. They came to anchor in the long sheltered bay that indents the southeast shore of St. Joseph Island, and there they established the settlement, complete with sawmill and store. Rains named it Milford Haven, for the scene of his happy childhood summers in Wales.

But all was not happy in the new Milford Haven. Few additional settlers came, and Rains, the major financial backer of the enterprise, ran out of money when his London agent managed to lose £30,000 in investments that went sour. He quarreled with his partners, and, disgusted by his first venture into business, decided to withdraw from the company and go it alone. He built a new home about ten miles west of the settlement, on a promontory that became known as Rains Point.

It would be more accurate to say he built two homes. Even before they left Lake Simcoe, Eliza, the devoted sister and aunt, had become the loving consort. By now the parties to this *ménage à trois* were completely open and candid about their private arrangement. Apparently it satisfied them all. The sisters, devoted to one another, were quite willing to share a husband, who was devoted to both of them. Each enjoyed the role of mistress in her own home and direct supervision of her children. Among the three of them they educated a combined total of nineteen youngsters. Rains maintained an extensive library for the purpose.

Nor was the Canadian Government unduly outraged by Rains' personal life. As he had done on Lake Simcoe, he served as magistrate for Algoma District for many years. By 1860 he was beginning to feel those years and retired from his business supplying wood to steamers on St. Marys River. He died in 1874 at the age of 85. His improprieties forgotten or overlooked, Major Rains was buried at Sault Ste. Marie with full military honors. Although his story has faded into legend, every boat that cruises St. Mary's River, or moves northeast between Drummond and St. Joseph Islands into the North Channel, encounters his memory in the places he named, and in the places named for him—Rains Point, Rains Lake, and Rains Wharf Range.

Anchorage

When you round the flashing red light on Koshkawong Point to enter Milford Haven, you'll understand why Major Rains chose it for the site of his settlement. The long, narrow bay is comfortably sheltered from wind and sea, and its wooded banks, with just a few cottages visible, are warm and friendly. The best spot to anchor is on the northwest side of Sandy Point in ten to twelve feet.

Hilton Beach
Charts 2250 and 2251

St. Joseph Island is mostly level, which makes it good for the farming that has been its mainstay for most of the past 100 years since the timber was logged off. One of the few places where hills rise from the plain is near the northeast corner. On one exploring trip to this part of the island Major Rains and his sons lost their bearings. When they finally emerged from the woods after a weary night, they had to climb up and over several large hills to reach the shore. What better name for this place, the Major decided, than Hill Town. The name stuck. After settlers began to arrive in the 1850s, not a Hilton among them, they transformed it into the even more descriptive Hilton Beach.

Approach

Hilton Beach lies about fifteen miles around the eastern end of St. Joseph Island from Milford Haven. At the green spar east of Koshkawong Point you can turn northeast to pass between two pairs of islands, Beef and Hog on the port hand, O'Donnell and Colville to starboard. Fox Island, ahead of you, should be left to port, however. Mind long South Bank extending from it. Moffat Bay, a few miles farther on the route, offers a possible anchorage, especially on its eastern side where there are only scattered cottages, but the bay is open to northwest through northeast winds.

From Gravel Point, where you enter St. Joseph Channel proper, the white obelisk war memorial in the shoreside park at Hilton Beach identifies the village and guides you toward the government dock with a fixed red light on the old freight shed. But note the green spar on Fisher Shoal and give it a good berth.

Dockage and Marine Services

A dredged basin behind the L-shaped government wharf, entered from the east side, has one floating dock off the wharf side and several projecting from the shore side. Depths range from five to eight feet, but it doesn't really matter because in season there is not likely to be any place at all for a transient boat. If you come in for gas (no diesel) you will moor to the outside of the government dock, which is not a good place to lie overnight. The outside of the stem of the L, however, on the northwest side of the structure, is in pretty good condition, and you could probably lie there comfortably. Electric power, fresh water, and pumpout are also provided by Hilton Beach Marine and Sports.

Activities for the Crew

Take ten minutes to tour the town. The general store is a couple of blocks from the dock, and on the way you'll pass the public library, and the shiny Harbourview Cafe, offering snacks and meals. The little waterfront park, with beach, playground, and roped off swim area, completes the amenities of Hilton Beach—tiny (210 people) and peaceful.

The Anchorages of Campement D'Ours
Chart 2250

Like the rock at the mouth of the cave, Campement D'Ours Island stands in the middle of St. Joseph Channel, about three miles from Hilton Beach. It is doubtful that there are bears on it anymore. No obstacle to be impatiently by-passed, this handsome island, almost a mile and a half square, is a destination itself. It cannot be circumnavigated by a cruising boat because of shoals and a low bridge, but Gawas Bay penetrates for about a mile and a half between its south side and the St. Joseph shore; the main channel runs north of it.

    The St. Joseph side of narrow Gawas Bay is thickly populated with cottages, but the Campement D'Ours side is quite wild. If the outboard traffic doesn't bother you unduly, there is pleasant anchorage to be had along that shore in four to nine feet. The bay itself carries no less than ten feet down the middle, but watch out for shoaling near the entrance around Canoe Point; stay 200 to 300 feet off.

Along the well-buoyed main channel around the east and north sides of Campement D'Ours Island,.there are some attractive homes on its shores. At the northwest point of the island, turn off the channel and move down between the splendid high cliffs of Campement D'Ours and Picture Islands. In a twinkling you'll feel far removed from the civilization you just turned away from. The water is very deep here, but anchorage can be managed if you can make the agonizing choice between two tantalizing coves. Cleft into the rocks of Campement D'Ours Island is an unnamed little bight that is thirty feet deep where there is sufficient room to swing. If you anchor on chain you can manage that safely; the other alternative is to tie off to trees at the end of the cove.

Across the way, between uninhabited Picture and Sapper Islands, some careful passes with the depth finder will locate depths as little as fifteen feet for anchorage. Whichever spot you choose you will be surrounded by the high rocks, embellished with rustling forest, that spells North Channel.

Richards Landing
Chart 2250

The fixed highway bridge lies two miles beyond the Campement D'Ours anchorages. If your boat is suitable you can go on another two and one-half miles to Richards Landing. The village is named for an early settler, John Richards.

Approach

St. Joseph Channel is quite closely buoyed at its northernmost point just east of the highway bridge, and as you move southwest toward Richards Landing there is a fixed red lighted rear range on a course of 233 degrees. Another set of buoys gets

GOVERNMENT DOCK AT RICHARD'S LANDING

you past some shoals on the final approach to the village. If you are entering St. Joseph Channel from St. Marys River, and therefore approaching Richards Landing from the west, there is a tricky, but well buoyed, pass to thread off Boulanger Point.

Dockage and Marine Services

The Government Dock at Richards Landing is of the classic design, sturdy wood extensions on either side of the old concrete wharf. Alongside tie-up on the inner face, in ten feet, is the location of choice. Electricity is available with long cables, as are water, pumpout and gasoline, all supplied by Paul's Marina. The original freight shed is now The Wharf Restaurant; that is where the heads are located.

Activities for the Crew

There is more walking to do around Richards Landing than there was at Hilton Beach. But of course it's a much bigger town—350 people. In addition to the grocery store and public library, there is a liquor store here, several restaurants, and the island's hospital. There is also Courtenay's Gift Shop with a choice collection of Canadian crafts, including jewelry made from the unusual local puddingstone. This jaspar conglomerate, the official name, is found on the shores and in fields all over the island; collecting it is a popular hobby. Next door to Courtenay's is the Lion's Club tennis court.

Killaly Cove
Chart 2250

From Richards Landing you can proceed to St. Marys River and continue to cruise elsewhere, or you can turn around for more of the North Channel. Retracing your track back under the bridge and to the northwest tip of Campement D'Ours Island, a spacious bay opens up on the port side around Killaly Point, named for an engineer on the St. Lawrence canals. Not as grand as the Campement D'Ours anchorages, it is, nevertheless, a pretty and lightly populated place. There is a cottage on each side of the entrance and one at the foot of the bay, but you can drop your hook out of visual range in front of the rock face in twenty feet or less. The point closes off for excellent shelter when you're placed there. Take care on entering Killaly Cove to avoid the rocks off the point itself.

Just east of Killaly Cove, at Kensington Point, Holder Marine supplies gas and has a small marine railway and repair services, if you are misfortunate enough to need them. There is also a launching ramp here.

At the turn of the century the land and colonization agent of the Canadian Pacific Railway, Mr. L.O. Armstrong, decided to promote this area as a resort. To publicize it he sent a group of Ojibways to Boston to invite the daughters of Henry Wadsworth Longfellow to a Pageant of Hiawatha he was preparing to stage in August on one of the islands. The Indians must have been persuasive because the three women and their husbands, along with several friends to make up a party of twelve, all trooped out to the wilds of Northern Ontario for the event. Armstrong built a stone lodge on the

PORTLOCK HARBOUR

island, aptly named Longfellow, to accommodate them. The name doesn't appear on the chart, nor are there any known critical reviews of the production.

Portlock Harbour
Chart 2250

The north shore of St. Joseph Channel didn't need much promotion to attract summer visitors. Portlock Harbour has been a favorite for several generations, but most of the cottages are well spaced and blend in with their surroundings, leaving scenic vistas for the cruising boat. Continuing along the channel east of Campement D'Ours Island, your course will be roughly southeast from the light on Plummer Bank. You're looking for a rather small pair of spar buoys, red and green, about two and one-half miles away. If you have trouble picking them up you can detour far enough south to get a good sight on the obelisk at Hilton Beach. A course of 030° from that (actually from the light, but the obelisk will do at this distance) should place you at the buoys. From there daybeacons guide you past Piercy Rocks and Woodman Point into landlocked Portlock Harbour.

There are two places where you can find secluded anchorage among the steeply wooded and rocky shores in six to ten feet. The first is between Portlock and Dawson Islands just beyond the entrance. There are no cottages on the Portlock side. We know that Dawson Island was named for S.E. Dawson, Member of Parliament who pushed the government to survey the area, but, oddly, it is uncertain who Portlock was. Perhaps the name is simply descriptive of a landlocked harbor. Proceeding deep into the harbor, a little under two miles from the entrance at Woodman Point, anchorage in the cove behind Wurtele Point will keep only one house in view.

Portlock Harbor is a delightful place to explore by dinghy. There is no safe passage through to St. Joseph Channel from the north end of the harbor for a cruising boat, but in the dinghy you can enjoy scenic circumnavigations of Dawson and Portlock Islands and their satellites. One is tempted to linger here, but other attractions await.

~Three ~

The North Shore

Along the North Shore of the North Channel the terrain varies from rolling farmland to thick forest to rugged rocky outcrop and bush, with a few lakes thrown in for emphasis. The towns that march in line are linked by Highway 17 and by the Canadian Pacific Railway. The hum of traffic, audible from the water, reminds you that you aren't very far from civilization, but the whistle of the trains rivals the call of the loon for lonesome mood music. And the towns remain small, slow-paced, and reminiscent of the gentle life of the old days.

Bruce Mines
Charts 2550 and 2251

When North America's first mining boom was launched on Michigan's copper range in the 1840s, it set off a scramble of exploration throughout the upper Great Lakes. In 1846 one James Cuthbertson located a vein of copper at what is today the village of Bruce Mines. He sold his claim to the Montreal Mining Company, and they shipped out the first load of ore in 1847. Bruce Mines was the first of a bonanza of mining locations in northern Ontario that would, over ensuing decades, wrest an alchemist's array of valuable minerals from deep in the earth. For thirty years the Bruce Mines flourished, but by the late 1870s they were no longer profitable, and closed. One of the last managers was no less a personage than Lord Percy Douglas, Marquis of Queensbury. Not the boxing Marquis—that was his father. In fact he didn't succeed to the title until he returned to England in .1900. But he left behind at Bruce Mines his illustrious name, the house he is believed to have occupied, and his daughter's doll house on display in the museum.

Approach

Bruce Mines lies just beyond the eastern end of St. Joseph Channel. If you are coming from there, make sure to identify the red spar on McKay Reef and keep clear; it stands surprisingly far off shore. Approaching from the south or east the red spar on Prout Rock is the one to watch out for. In any case, a church spire in the village helps to identify its location from offshore. The old McKay Island lighthouse, now a private home, is more conspicuous than the light and daymark itself. The channel is buoyed into the marina, which has a flashing red light on the dock.

Dockage and Marine Services

The Bruce Mines Marina has floating docks laid perpendicular to a long pier thrusting from shore. Dockage for service is on the west side of the L-shaped terminus of this pier, and the berths are also entered from the west. These are not individual slips, as most of the docks accommodate two boats, so tieup is actually alongside, rather than in wells. Depths range from six to ten feet. Gasoline, diesel fuel, pumpout, fresh water, electricity (mostly 20-amp outlets with a couple of 30-amp at the innermost docks), heads and showers are all provided. The showers have an unusual faucet that must be pushed to obtain water, which is dispensed at a set temperature on a timer.

Activities for the Crew

Everything is very conveniently located in this village of 625 people. At the head of the road leading to the dock is K's Motel and restaurant. Supermarket, liquor store, bank, post office, laundromat, and gift shops are all right on the main street. The hardware store is a couple of miles away at Bruce Station, but there are taxis. For amusement as well as good food, try the Bear Trap restaurant. Furnished with a kitschy array of antiques, its menu expresses the proprietor's joy in rhyming and punning.

Entertainment other than eating consists mainly of tennis on the town court, walking, and a visit to the Bruce Mines Museum. Housed in an 1894 church with an unusual Norman tower, the museum contains interesting artifacts and memorabilia belonging to the Cornish men and their families who were brought over 125 years ago or more to work the mines. On your walk follow the coast road around from the museum for about a mile, and you'll come to the impressive mansion that is said to have belonged to Lord Douglas. Regrettably, it's not in very good shape, and an incongruous modern addition has been attached to the front for a bar.

THE LORD DOUGLAS HOUSE, BRUCE MINES

With its convenient shopping and ample ramp and parking facilities, Bruce Mines is a good place to launch a trailered boat for exploration of St. Joseph Channel. Greyhound bus service through town also makes it handy to receive and discharge boat guests here.

Macbeth Bay
Chart 2251

A passage of twelve miles from Bruce Mines brings you to Thessalon Point, a long finger of land (that, in fact, is what the name means), which has guided lake-faring men since the first frail birch bark canoe was launched in the dimness of unrecorded history. It is identified by a red and white daymark, topped by a flashing white light.

On leaving Bruce Mines it is best to lay a southeast course to the south side of Cedar Island, and then due east to Thessalon Point, in order to avoid the bank of unmarked shoals between Birch and Larry Islands. Close northwest of the point Macbeth Bay affords pleasant anchorage along this coast with few bays that are both sheltered and unobstructed. The long peninsula of Thessalon Point is the guide to its approach. From about half a mile west of the point, head due north for Bald Rock (you'll know it when you see it), then pass between that one and Gereaux Rock to port. Keep closer to Gereaux (about 150 yards off) and gradually swing northwest, leaving about the same distance to the little unnamed island northeast of Gooseberry Island, which is also left to port. Note: in the very high water of 1986 Gereaux Rock was barely breaking, but the island off Gooseberry was clearly visible. This whole passage should carry a minimum of 12 feet at chart datum.

The resort and beach on the eastern end of Macbeth Bay may seem a bit raucous, but as you move westward down the middle you'll find only one house on the Chevalier Islands and none on the mainland opposite them. Anchor behind the eastern Chevalier Island in six to ten feet. At the western end of the west Chevalier Island and on Frechette and the island in between there are good rock landings for a dinghy or small boat. You can exit the anchorage between Frechette Island and the unnamed island west of it, especially if you're headed west, watching out for the shoals around Africa Rock. But because Frechette is so hard to identify from seaward it is not a good idea to try to enter that way.

Thessalon
Chart 2251

As an example of urban architecture, Thessalon isn't much to look at, but on the short walk from the dock to the village you get a close-up view of the natural architecture of the North Channel. Great slabs of glacier-scoured rock thrust up from the thin stony soil. Harebells and daisies take root in the crevices and nod a friendly greeting to passersby.

Lumber gave Thessalon its original reason for existence when Nathanael Dyment build the first sawmill in the 1870s, although almost 100 years before that it narrowly missed becoming the British military headquarters on the upper Great Lakes. (The British decided, instead, to stay on at Mackinac Island, despite the 1783 Treaty of Paris which placed it in U.S. territory.) When the halcyon days of the lumberjack receded into memory, the town slipped into a genteel shabbiness from which it has now emerged with vigor. Birchland Veneer Mill, back of the harbor, maintains the wood products tradition, and its staff is hospitable to visitors. It's well worth the walk over to watch the birch logs ascend the chute, slide along to the great cutting blades, and then get peeled like onions as they are rolled over and over until reduced to a lollipop stick core.

The other major industry in Thessalon is tourism. Across the bridge over the Thessalon River and on the west side of the peninsula lie the sand beaches and the motels and tourist campground to populate them. Thessalon's location just off Trans-Canada Highway 17 fifty miles east of Sault Ste. Marie, and the availability of motels and supply facilities make it a good jumping-off place for trailer boats. The major island cruising grounds are about 35 miles east, however, so small boats without sufficient power to cruise at least ten to fifteen miles an hour over open water should not set off from here.

For the slower little boats there is an appealing island group closer to hand and plenty of semi-wild shoreline to explore close eastward from town, while the Thessalon River is unspoiled and navigable for about five miles to the first rapids. In addition, Thessalon is the gateway to a fabulous world of inland lakes—a few have rustic resorts on them, but many more are uninhabited. All are reputed to be happy fishing grounds, and enough of them are accessible by dirt road to offer plenty of choice

Highway 129, north from Thessalon, is spectacularly scenic as it follows the Mississagi River. Sixty-five miles up is Aubrey Falls, where an enormous power dam has been so constructed as to leave much of the falls in a free flowing state amid natural surroundings that effectively screen from view the intrusion of modern technology. The land-based vacationer will find this a rewarding side trip, and the crew of a cruising boat might find a rental car at one of the auto dealers in town.

Approach

The approach to Thessalon Point from the west was described in the previous section. From the east there are no obstructions. Less than one-half mile east of the point a range, consisting of two white and orange daymarks, topped with fixed green lights, will bring you into the harbor on a heading of 022°. The channel is buoyed to carry you safely past the rubble and rock slab breakwater on the starboard side to the government dock. But take care not to confuse the daymark on the flashing red breakwater light for the front range. The front range light is on the government wharf.

Dockage and Marine Services

The concrete, L-shaped government dock offers good protection from all directions. There are floating piers on the inside faces for alongside tieup in twelve to fourteen feet. Anchorage is ill advised, as the harbor is generally foul except where dredged out for dockage.

Gas, diesel, block ice, water, propane, pumpout, heads and showers are available at Bill's Marina on the landward end of the dock. Electric power can be had anywhere along the dock face, some locations requiring longer cable than others. Bill sells charts and will provide mechanical assistance and arrange haulout if you need it. The launch ramp is near the dock.

Activities for the Crew

Thessalon has fewer than 1,600 residents, but it supports two good supermarkets, a bakery, a couple of hardware stores, government liquor store, a bank, a pharmacy, clothing, jewelry, and gift shops, and the best laundromat on the North Channel. Doctors of medicine and dentistry and a hospital are all available should you need them. Greyhound bus service and the airstrip five miles from town make Thessalon a convenient place to pick up and discharge guests on cruising boats.

To accommodate its growing tourist industry, Thessalon has three motels and a campground within the town limits, all located along the waterfront on the west side. (There are many more lodges, resorts, and campgrounds in the surrounding district.) The Golden Rooster and Belle Isle motels are modest; the Carolyn Beach Motel is the largest and best appointed. Across the road The Cache features fine English and Canadian gifts and artwork.

The Golden Rooster and the Carolyn Beach have nice dining rooms. They present a fair walk from the dock, a mile and a mile and a half respectively, but there are taxis if you want to get up there for dinner. Right downtown the Skyway Restaurant serves Chinese food, and there are a couple of additional lunch and snack places. The Farmhouse, six miles east of town, is a charming restaurant associated with the excellent Round Barn Canadian craft shop. It offers a more sophisticated menu than is commonly found on the North Channel, and will provide transportation from the dock for boating guests.

On the main street there are two hotels with cocktail bars, dating from the not-so-long-ago time when Ontario liquor licensing laws permitted only hotels to serve alcoholic beverages. For a more edifying pastime, the public library opens three afternoons and four evenings a week. The community hall runs a bingo game one or two nights a week; check in town for the schedule.

East Grant Island
Chart 2251

En route eastbound, you will pass East Grant Island, thickly wooded, with cobble beaches around its large bay. From the chart the harbor appears to be wide open to the northwest, but there is sheltered anchorage for two or three cruising yachts (more, if tied off to trees), in ten to twenty feet over mud, between Fishery Island and the northwest shore of East Grant. Enter this anchorage only from the East Grant bay; do not come in directly from the north. The shoal draft boat can beach in a number of locations among the Grant Island group, only fifteen miles from Thessalon.

Crew members who remember their history may be interested to know that these islands are named for Lieutenant John Grant, who commanded the British gunboat *Confiance*. Originally American, *Confiance* was built at Erie, Pennsylvania and christened *Tigress*, to serve admirably in Oliver Hazard Perry's Lake Erie fleet during the War of 1812. But in September, 1814, while patrolling at the mouth of St. Marys River, she was captured by a brave and ingenious British naval officer (Worsley, not Grant) and renamed when she went into His Majesty's Service. Under Grant's command she served during the early 1820s as the British headquarters ship for the International Boundary Commission.

The French Islands
Chart 2251

A few miles beyond the Grant Islands, the French Islands enclose Mississagi Bay. It is ironic that in this region of mostly Indian and English place names these little islands are among the few whose titles pay tribute to the French who came first—but to Frenchmen who rarely or never plied these waters! The bold René Robert Cavelier, Sieur de la Salle, earned his fame elsewhere, as did his sidekick, boastful, gregarious Father Louis Hennepin, and his friend, the shrewd Henri de Tonty. Certainly imperious Cardinal Richelieu never saw this place. But if you decide to enter Mississagi Bay you will pass close to Talon Rock. There was a gentleman who deserved more of a memorial here than a tiny hunk of stone three and a half feet high. Intendent of New France during the mid-seventeenth century, Jean Talon encouraged exploration of the West and the opening of the Great Lakes country to fur trading and mining.

A cruising boat will have no reason to enter wide and shallow Mississagi Bay; unfortunately, there is no anchorage here with any protection at all from the west. On the other hand, a small, shallow draft boat can be beached or tied off to shore in a number of spots where it will be safe from bouncing. Its occupants may then find a picturesque campsite, especially on Tonty and Hennepin Islands, with a large bay and the Mississagi River to fish and explore.

Blind River
Charts 2252, 2259, and 2268

Like Thessalon, Blind River is a town that lumber built, only here it built bigger and more prosperously. At one time there were seven lumber companies operating. When the first mill was built in 1878, the Hudson's Bay Company was still trading for furs at its Blind River post. By the time the post was closed in 1905 the town had hit its stride in lumber. Many of the early lumbermen of the North Channel came from Michigan, to cut the pine and float it in huge rafts down the lake to their mills. Later, when the Canadian government imposed an embargo on raw logs, these Americans began to build sawmills in Ontario. Russell Alger, who had been Governor of Michigan in 1885-86, was one of these, although he departed Blind River when President William McKinley appointed him Secretary of War in 1897. Michigan's influence on Blind River is perpetuated to this day in the name of the town's main street, Woodward Avenue.

The most colorful character associated with the town's early history, and one of its most influential citizens, was a native Canadian, James J. McFadden. After a short career as a bartender he got into the logging business in the 1880s, arriving on the North Channel about 1908. In his first large operation he is reported to have bought the whole town of Spragge and its sawmill for $50,000. Then, in the fall of 1919, he bought the big mill that had been built in 1902 on the west side of the harbor at Blind River by the Eddy brothers of Saginaw, Michigan. Shrewd in the bidding for timber rights whenever the government opened up another township for sale, J.J. could also turn a neat profit in the exchange of private property. In 1926 he sold this mill, and all the timber rights on the Mississagi River that went with it, to a Minneapolis firm for $3 million.

Keeping the McFadden name, the new firm built a more modern facility that was reputed to be the largest sawmill east of the Rocky Mountains, then sold out in 1932. Four years later McFadden bought his mill back again, this time from receivership, at just $300,000. In effect, he paid nothing for the mill because there was an estimated $300,000 worth of logs waiting in the booming area. One more time J.J. McFadden sold his mill for $3 million. That was in 1942, when he retired to live out the remaining ten years of his life in his handsome lakeside home just east of town. Meanwhile the mill, officially known as the McFadden Branch, became part of the large Dom-Tar Company and the sole survivor of Blind River's once flourishing lumber industry. Finally, in 1969, it closed for the last time. Little remains of the buildings and nothing of the machinery. But from far off at sea, the tall, dome-topped burner still looms against the sky, guiding the mariner into a safe harbor.

Approach

That safe harbor, in fact, is precisely where the booming ground used to be. On the approach to Blind River from the

west, 32 miles from Thessalon, the only hazard is Patrick
Point Bank, which extends over a mile offshore, but is marked
by a green spar. No obstructions lie on the eastern or
southern approach until you reach Belle Rock, marked by a
red spar. The extensive Blind River Bank, which fronts this
whole stretch of coast, is quite shallow, however, and there
are some spots with only four feet of water at chart datum.
Comb Point is equipped with a lighted daymark, and from
here you follow a buoyed channel right into the marina in
Dorothy Inlet. The ruined piles and dolphins still shown on
chart 2268 have been removed.

Dockage and Marine Services

The Blind River Marina, operated by Don and Sue Francis, is
an attractive one with helpful service. The floating docks for
alongside tieup in ten foot lie perpendicular to a long pier
extending from shore. The service area for gas, diesel, and
pumpout is on the inside end of the line of slips. Electricity
and water are available at each dock. At the head of the pier
is the head and shower building, with ice and a small marine
store that also sells charts. A travel lift can haul to 75 feet, with
boat and motor repair services obtainable through the
Francises. They also offer bicycle and car rental and operate
Freedom Yacht Charters with boats in the 25- to 35-foot
range. The marina monitors channel 68.

Activities for the Crew

With over 3,500 residents, Blind River is the largest town on
the North Channel. At one time it was considerably larger, but
as the lumber mills began to close in the 1920s and 1930s, it
went into a decline. Then in the mid-1950s the discovery of
uranium and the opening of several mines at Elliot Lake, a
mere 35 miles away, gave the town new jobs and life. Since
then the well-being of many Blind River families has fluctu-
ated with the demand for uranium, while the ubiquitous
tourist has provided an important measure of stability.

For the visitor by boat, a pleasant half-mile walk leads downtown, where there are several grocery stores, including a supermarket, a meat market, and a bakery. If you have a yen for fresh fish, turn right at Jetty Street and walk one block to the dock at the outlet of the Blind River (known locally as Carlson's Dock) to see what's available at Carlson's Fishery.

CARLSON'S DOCK, BLIND RIVER

The Carlson brothers have fished out of the Blind River since their father moved here from Spragge in 1948, in order to obtain electric power for the family and better schooling for his children. Their catch moves out quickly to feed New York and Boston within 36 hours, although in many other places on the North Channel the commercial fish tug has gone the way of the beaver trapline and the two-handed saw.

Continuing downtown, the usual complement of stores is to be found—drug, clothing, jewelry, gift, hardware, liquor, and banks. There is a laundromat (two, in fact), but not conveniently located for travelers on foot. In addition to car rental at the marina, however, there are taxis to carry your laundry and your heavy purchases. Greyhound bus service offers good possibilities for crew changes. And, should you need it, there is a modern hospital that you pass on your way from the marina.

For daytime entertainment, the Timber Village Museum, on Highway 17 at the eastern edge of town about a mile and a half from the marina, tells artfully of the region's lumbering history. The exquisite craftsmanship of Joseph Briere's wood carvings are a special attraction. A mile and a half the other way from the marina is Huron Pines nine-hole golf course, and there are tennis courts in town. Riverside Beach and playground offer outdoor recreation for children of all ages, and Seller's Beach is directly on the North Channel.

As a commentary on Blind River's destiny, one of the four motels in town sits on the dam site of the first sawmill. It is, of course, the Old Mill Motel. The Edgewater Inn, Vajda's Motel, and the North Shore Motel have restaurants. Another good bet for dinner is the 17 Restaurant, where Chinese food is featured. To top off your evening in Blind River, you can take in a movie at the Palace Theatre. Community Days in early July is the major summer event, with a parade, contests, and street dancing, among other activities.

Serpent Harbour (Spragge)
Charts 2252, 2259, and 2268

In days gone by Blind River had a sister city. About fifteen miles east, Spragge boomed in the early days of the present century, with its whining sawmills and the 'jacks coming out of the woods to raise hell on a Saturday night. (Did they know that the scene of their revelry was named for a sober chief justice of Ontario?) The moves of men like McFadden and Carlson give a clue to Spragge's fate. Today virtually nothing marks the spot but a cluster of houses, an old railroad station, and a single highway sign to tell you you're there if you look fast enough. But down the side road from the signpost on Highway 17 is something different.

On that side road is a fork. One branch leads to Spragge's attempt at a new life—the Pronto uranium mine, with the remains of a burned head frame, some outbuildings, and old borings lying around on the slag heaps that glitter with fool's gold and silver. The place is hushed and deserted. High hopes for a few years, and then it became uneconomic to dig for an ore that was too lean to pay for the trouble.

The other branch of the fork leads to a clearing on Herman Point (Herman Cook was an M.P. from the Lake Simcoe area) at the mouth of the Serpent River. Here the North Channel Yacht Club—the only yacht club for 100 miles and more in any direction—has been carved from the bush by a group of dedicated, industrious, hospitable devotees of the nautical way of life. Sailors and power boatmen alike, they have come from Elliot Lake, Sudbury, and points east and west to build the place with their bare hands and to ride the winds and waves of their beloved North Channel. Nothing pretentious, but a warm welcome, a helping hand, and a spirit of camaraderie are offered to visiting boats.

Approach

Whether approaching from the west, east, or south, the Reiss Lime Company cement plant stack conspicuously identifies the entrance to Serpent River and Harbour. A course of 068° from the northeast tip of Round Island (high and conspicuous), carried just under four miles from the island tip, will clear the islands and shoals in the river mouth and bring you to Meteor Rock. Note that chart 2259 shows a buildup of land leading from the Reiss Lime plant to Strong Island; this does not show up well from the water and Strong Island looks like an island.

At a point midway between the second Fournier Island and Meteor Rock, turn northward to clear Meteor, then northeastward again to pass close to Narrow Point and so avoid the shoal water extending from the north shore. Note the submerged wreck just beyond Narrow Point and the rock just east of the fingers of land projecting from the old village site. Before the road was built small 80-foot ships brought in mail and supplies. One caught fire while docked at Spragge, was cut loose, and drifted across the waterway to Nobles Island, where it burned to the waterline and sank. A course midway between the mainland and the northernmost points of Nobles Island should avoid both of these hazards until Herman Point is rounded for entrance to the yacht club.

Dockage and Marine Services

Most of the yacht club boats are kept on moorings in the harbor, but there are floating docks with ten-foot depths alongside used by some of them. Space is often available for a visiting boat from Monday to Thursday, when few members are about. The resident caretaker will direct you to a dock location or the vacant mooring of a club member away on holiday. The club is unable to accommodate visitors at all on weekends.

Gasoline, diesel, 30-amp electric power, pumpout, ice, and water are available at the dock, with heads and showers in a separate building. The clubhouse is not open to transient visitors. A marine railroad can haul out boats to 35 feet in length. There are no marine mechanics, as such, in the area, but club members could probably obtain a diesel mechanic through one of the mines. There is a car park and launch ramp for trailered boats.

Activities for the Crew

Informal association with other people "messing about with boats" provides one form of shoreside entertainment. The mine is fenced and locked, but the whole area offers interesting possibilities for the rock hound. If an opportunity presents itself to get a ride to Elliot Lake, you should take it. A modern, planned city that sprang full blown from the forested hills in 1955, it languished for a while with the demand for uranium, but is now on the upswing of its fortune cycle. The Mining and Nuclear Museum tells a fascinating story. Closer at hand there is a cemetery to explore back in the bush, with headstones dating back 100 years.

The Serpent River is navigable by dinghy for a considerable distance into the interior. It is mostly wild and parts of it are quite scenic. Although Serpent Harbour itself is not of great interest to trailer boats and boat campers, those who like river exploration will find here one of the longest navigable streams in the area. The next bend is always tantalizing. And this is one of the few places along the North Channel where canoeists can ply their paddles in safety from the high winds and seas that might spring up.

Spragge offers another place at which to pick up and discharge boat guests by public transportation, as Greyhound will stop on demand. It also provides excellent access to the islands of the North Channel for trailered boats.

Nobles Island Anchorage

Whether or not dockage or a mooring is obtainable, you can enjoy the conviviality of the club from the vantage of a beautiful anchorage a mere three quarters of a mile dinghy ride away. From the club point head 174° for about three tenths of a mile, passing the two Morrison Islands. (Morrison was an Owen Sound lawyer.) When the passage between Nobles Island and the mainland opens up abeam to starboard, taking care to avoid the rock off the southeast tip of Nobles, turn and steer down the middle into an imposing, high-walled sanctuary. Anchor in eight to twelve feet over sand wherever it suits your fancy, except in the shallow, weedy bight on the south side. When you're ready to depart this peaceful place, named for a Manitoulin fish merchant, go right on through the western opening, again steering midway through the narrows, to find yourself on the south (exit) side of Meteor Rock, ready to leave Serpent Harbour the way you came in.

Spanish
Charts 2252, 2257, and 2268

Beyond Spragge Highway 17 deserts the shores of the North Channel; there are no more towns on the waterway for another eighteen miles as the crow flies, until the highway comes close again at Spanish. Initially a lumber town, like all its neighbors, the origin of its name lies in mildly controversial obscurity. Some say a Spaniard fled the hand of justice on the lower Mississippi in the old fur trade days, when New Orleans was an outpost of the Kings of Castille. He ended up among the noninquisitive *coureurs de bois* and so gave a name to this place and the river on which it sits.

On the other hand, Sarah Owl, who came from a very long-lived family, told some years back of how her great grandfather participated in an Ojibway raid far to the south and brought back a Spanish woman as a prisoner. Helpless to return to her people, she married a brave who lived on the river and probably taught her children her native language. When Canadian voyageurs met up with these Spanish speaking Indians, they naturally identified the area by that phenomenon. There are still people in the neighborhood surnamed Espaniel.

Spanish River, about 21 miles from the Serpent, may or may not appeal to the crew of a shallow draft boat. Although scenic, it is none too clean, and if the wind is right you can identify the source of pollution almost thirty miles up at Espanola's (the same Spaniard?) giant paper mill. But a trailer boat crew, who found Thessalon or Blind River too far from the islands, might want to launch at Spanish for access to the anchorages along the Whalesback and McBean Channels.

There is really only one reason why a cruising boat, and a shallow draft one at that, would haul itself into the mouth of Spanish River—it needs something, and Spanish is the last town on the north shore for thirty miles eastward. There are no amenities, either natural or man made, to recommend the place.

Approach

The approach to Spanish from the Whalesback Channel is clear and free of obstructions, provided you identify and count islands accurately. East of Buswell Point a flashing red light buoy marks the beginning of the buoyed channel to the dock. Caution: the channel is supposed to be dredged to four feet at chart datum, but continuous silting of the river has reduced it to two to three feet in places. The channel rather dramatically contrasts the rocky, pine-studded terrain of its north bank with the marshy reed beds stretching across the shallow river on the south.

Dockage and Marine Services

The government dock is identified by the picturesque lighthouse replica on shore. It is of the planked variety, with wood tieup rail and five to seven feet of depth. It is a small dock to serve a small place, without services.

Gasoline can be obtained at Vance's Marina, a short distance upstream, where there is also a launch ramp. Mitchell's Camp, next door to the government dock, has a launch ramp and head and shower room. Both camps, which dock local boats, are rather elderly and minimal in their facilities.

Activities for the Crew

The town is located on Highway 17, one mile from the river front. Taxis are available, but the town isn't much more than a few stores strung along a bleak highway. The merchants are accommodating, however. Their services are listed on a bulletin board at the government dock—grocery stores, hardware, liquor and beer stores, bank, post office, hotel (bar), and a laundromat a half mile out of town to the east. Two of the groceries will deliver. The same Greyhound bus that passes through Thessalon stops at Spanish on demand, for transportation east or west.

If you continue east by car you will leave the North Channel, not to return for over forty miles until you turn south on Route 6 at Espanola. Should you seek accommodations along this scenic way, Massey, thirteen miles from Spanish, is a good place, with four motels and an interesting historical museum. Route 553 north from Massey leads to Chutes Provincial Park, and other roads branch out to numerous inland lakes. Four miles after you've turned south on Route 6,

Espanola, although often redolent of paper mill, offers more than a half dozen motels to choose from. With almost 6,000 residents, it is the largest town between Sault Ste. Marie and Sudbury, and it sports a nine-hole golf course, public swimming pool, tennis courts, bowling alley, and movies.

Enough of towns. Towns are for busyness, reminders of the chores and frustrations we left behind. The real North Channel is still waiting.

~Four ~

The North Channel of the North Channel

It begins just east of Blind River—that chain of magical isles that creates a little North Channel of its own. Here the cruising boat, large or small, can meander through channels worthy of the approach to Elysium, can anchor near or tie up to bold cliffs of rock or soft, mysterious forest. Here the crew will hear nothing but their own voices and the cry of the loon, the squawk of the gull, and the evensong of the whippoorwill. The sun warms the flat rocks for dozing after a cool swim in a quiet cove, the fish jump at night and play games with a ball of twine by day, the blueberries hide in the crevices of the hills of stone, and the wind ruffles the pines and makes them sing. In the islands is the serenity of a lazy summer afternoon, the comfort of a snug harbor while the seas may roar outside, the grandeur of the west wind piling up the clouds into thunderheads above, the witchery of a full moon gliding silently above the black tree points. In the islands is the stuff of dreams. . . .

Sanford (Clara) and Turnbull
Charts 2252 and 2259

Less than ten miles east of Blind River is the first group of cruising islands, named by the two largest ones. The names of all these islands give a rather personal touch to the locale, although many of the choices seem unrelated. Furthermore, the names have been switched around over the years in a geographic game of "Who's on First?" The western anchor of the archipelago was originally named Sanford, for a senator from Hamilton, and the island northwest of it across South Passage was called Gibson, for a lieutenant-governor of Ontario. For decades, however, the charts showed the name Clara, wife of W.J. Stewart, chief hydrographer of Canada, on Senator Sanford's island, while he replaced Gibson, and Gibson was left out in the cold.

The Elliot Lake attorney, who received the then-named Clara in settlement of a legal fee, being in the habit of verifying things like titles, discovered the error. It took him perhaps twenty years to persuade the federal government to correct the mistake. The newer charts have at last restored the original Sanford to the long-time Clara and the original Gibson to the formerly usurped Sanford. Now it is Clara who is left out in the cold, although her husband's sister, Caroline, remains in situ.

The other names seem to be fixed in their heavens. Vaux was a Hamilton lawyer and probably executor of Sanford's estate. James F. Turnbull, a lieutenant-colonel in the Royal Canadian Dragoons, Georgian Bay steamer captain Bassett, Simon J. Dawson, M.P., Emile Doucet, district engineer of the National Transcontinental Railway, Peter Scott, a naval surveyor, and a British gunboat named *Cherub* don't appear to have had a great deal in common in their earlier incarnations, but they shall be forever associated geographically by their namesakes. Who was Jane? History seems to have forgotten.

Sanford Island is rather low and wooded, with a lovely home on its south shore. Uninhabited Turnbull, connected to Bassett, has bluffs to climb and woods to soften them. Turnbull also has the most protected anchorage, dotted with

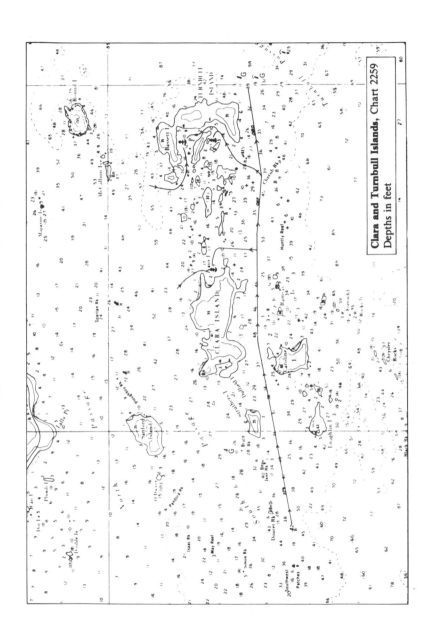

Clara and Turnbull Islands, Chart 2259

Depths in feet

numerous satellite islands to explore. There are berries to pick in season, a variety of rocks to collect, sand beaches in low water, and a great deal of bird life to observe. The sunsets from Turnbull harbor can be spectacular. The entire shoal upon which these two large and many small islands rest is populated by pike and bass.

Approach

The approach to these islands is buoyed from the southwest and the open part of the North Channel, rather than from Blind River. If you are coming from there, a course of 113° from the red spar buoy at Belle Rock should lead you safely past Simon Rock, showing four feet high at chart datum, and between Doucet Rock and the green spar southwest of it. Then steer a course of 079° from the green to enter the passage south of Sanford. Note the beacons on Doucet Rock and Jane Rock on your port side, make sure you have each island identified from the chart as you pass, and keep the depth sounder going. When you are in the center of the channel between Sanford and Caroline, continue on an easterly course until you pass the tip of the southeast hook of Sanford. From there a course of 097° will carry you safely past the underwater rocks north of Cherub Rock, which is visible eight feet high and backed up by high Scott Island. Just before Cherub Rock comes abeam, however, reshape your course either to enter Turnbull harbor or to pass on through on a heading of about 080° to the green spar marking Turnbull's southeast shoal and Turnbull Passage. If you are approaching from the east or south, clear sailing brings you to Turnbull's southeast green spar; from there, directions are simply reversed.

Anchorages

The best anchorage at Sanford Island is in the eastern bight between Sanford and Vaux Islands. After passing the southeast hook of Sanford, which has a wide sand beach, continue on the easterly course until midway between the small island close to the eastern tip of Sanford and the pair of tiny islands east of it. Then turn north into the anchorage and drop your hook through seven feet of water into mud. The anchorage can also be entered from the north by favoring Sanford Island in the deep water passage between its northeast tip and the four-foot high rocks lying northeast of it.

Shallow draft small boats can proceed directly from here eastward into Turnbull harbor and find anchorage or tieup almost anywhere among the numerous small islands. These islands also offer many choices for camping, although Turnbull, itself, is rather steep and densely wooded.

Larger cruising boats must enter Turnbull on a northerly course from Cherub Rock. As you enter the harbor, keep the group of low rocks marking the entrance to starboard. Once they are abeam, gradually swing around them so as to avoid the shoal making out a considerable distance from the island off your port bow. Good holding in twelve feet over mud can be had between Turnbull, the long island west of its middle, and the island marked "8" on the chart. Note the shoal extending southeast of the last named.

The chart shows only two feet of depth in the passage between Turnbull and the long, narrow island just west of its center. Actually, in all but very low water years, at least six feet can be carried through to an appealing anchorage in the shelter of Bassett Island's south shore. There are several deadheads to watch for in this passage, but plenty of room between them. The Bassett anchorage can also be entered from the north by rounding the high, steep-to island and its southwestern satellite just west of Bassett Island. The three-foot shoal shown extending southwest from Bassett is not as large as indicated, and there is ample room between Bassett and the two-foot high rock southwest of it to pass into the anchorage within 25 feet of the island's shore.

Long Point Cove
Chart 2259

Less than four miles northeast of Turnbull Passage lies a superb anchorage in the unnamed bay behind Long Point on the mainland shore, just outside the Serpent River mouth. Its devotees call it Long Point Cove. Possessed of all the graces of a North Channel anchorage—scenic vistas, rocks to climb and swim from, blueberries to pick, fish to catch, and perfect shelter from all winds—it takes a little navigating to get into.

Approaching from Turnbull Passage, take a course of 038° from the green spar off the southeast point of Turnbull Island to a position from which the Reiss Lime Company stack bears 010° Similarly if approaching from the west between Bassett Island and Round Island. If you're coming from the east through the Whalesback, pass around conspicuous Prendergast Island until the stack lines up at 010° At this point a course of 090° will take you along the south side of Navy Island. At the southeastern tip of Navy bear 115° to pass between the two unnamed islands south of it, then straighten up again at 090° along the south side of the eastern one of those. After about half a mile the anchorage entrance will open up on the starboard side. Do not confuse it with the deep bight in the island on the west side of the entrance. There is a minimum of thirteen feet through the middle of the entrance, but favor the starboard side.

The west end of the cove offers the more scenic location in a minimum of five feet over mud. The trick is to move just far enough down to screen the lime plant from view, without running aground. The east end has good holding, too, and the impressive bluff at the entrance, but the far end here is weedy. Depending on water level, there is sometimes a good swimming rock on the southeast side of the cove. There are also several dinghy landing places, but Long Point doesn't lend itself well to shoreside camping.

John Island and Its Neighbors
Charts 2252 and 2259

Once upon a time there were four brothers named Moiles. They were not noted for success in business. In fact, their sawmill at DeTour, Michigan was heavily in debt to the

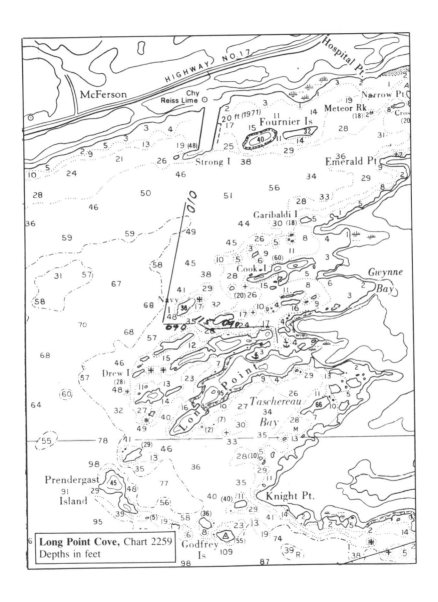

Long Point Cove, Chart 2259
Depths in feet

owners of the timber limits that supplied it with logs. With expenses so high, there was little hope of paying off the debt, let alone getting rich. Little hope, that is, until Bart came up with his brilliant idea. The 1890 season was just getting under way; the ice was only beginning to go out of St. Marys River. If the brothers didn't act quickly, this year would likely be as disastrous financially as last year had been, and they would lose everything.

When the boys arrived from Saginaw with two tugs and lighters, ostensibly to load lumber, they found their mill guarded by two watchmen in the employ of the ungenerously suspicious timber owners. Calling a cheerful greeting, the brothers entered their premises and remained all day behind closed doors and shaded windows. As evening fell, George emerged to commiserate with the man on guard duty about the boredom of his job, and offer him unexpected compensation in the form of a long-necked bottle. As the relief watch came on duty the liquid level was already moving down, and the happy guard retreated to his rooming house in anticipation of a warm and pleasant evening. The second man hadn't been at his post an hour when a breathless boy ran up to him with startling news: "Your missus' time has come. She sent word to town to fetch you home." The poor man, distracted by anxiety at the alarming prematurity of the event, was befriended by the sympathetic brothers. "Take our horse; we won't be needing it." Off at a gallop, the beast soon wound down to a slower and slower pace, eventually collapsing altogether with glazed eyes and the remarkable suggestion of a euphoric smile. The expectant father had no choice but to trudge on foot the last seven miles to his home, arriving too exhausted to return to duty after discovering the mistake.

Meanwhile, with no human eye to observe, interesting shadows passed through the night from mill to shore, fading away altogether in the very smallest hours of the new day. As dawn broke, the weary watchmen staggered back to the job only to discover there was nothing left to guard. Every bit of machinery, every stick of framing, every nail and screw was gone. The whole mill had been stolen! But Providence punishes the perpetrators of evil deeds. The temperature had dropped during the night, and there, just a few miles off shore, lay the nefarious flotilla—caught fast in the drifting ice. The jubilant guards ran to the telegraph office to send for the sheriff at Sault Ste. Marie. Outsmarted again by the cunning Bart, the wires had been cut.

Then began the breathless race. As horses galloped overland to fetch the law, the two tugs with their lighters in tow heaved and struggled through the ice, inching their perilous passage to the safety of the Canadian boundary. The race is not always to the swift. At 4:30 p.m. they crossed the finish line near Whiskey Point on St. Joseph Island. Early next day the intrepid sheriff of Chippewa County caught up with the fugitive tug under the command of John Moiles, again stuck fast in ice just over the border. The desperate John, fearful that the lawman would put a line on his tow and attempt to drag it back to U.S. waters, threatened mayhem with a rifle. Whereupon the sheriff, more prudent than brave, turned around and sailed home.

The desperadoes remained locked in the ice on the international boundary for three days, until a wind shift opened the way for them to call at the Canadian ports of Thessalon and Blind River. There the authorities welcomed them as investors in the future of the Canadian economy. Setting up shop in a central location on a beautiful island in the North Channel, they built a lumber wharf and cribwork for schooners. Logs towed across the North Channel from the forests of the Canadian north shore were fed into the maw and emerged as boards, shipped on the schooners that called. But the wages of sin are not high, and the boys never prospered here either. They sold out a few years later to Guy Multhorpe of Bay City, and when the timber gave out by World War I, the settlement was abandoned. Fire in 1918 finally destroyed the ghostly remains entirely. Only the names of John Island and its harbors survive to perpetuate the memory of the Moiles brothers. Though they never got rich, their thievery saved them from total obscurity. Yet even a part of their immortality was stolen—John happened to be the name of Lieutenant Bayfield's father, for whom he named the island seventy years before John Moiles arrived.

Approach

John Island, about five miles long, lies only seven miles east of Turnbull and ten miles from Spragge. Whether you are coming from the west or the east, directions to the two John Island harbors—John on the western end of the island and Moiles on the eastern—are the same. The approaches are clear and well buoyed.

Anchorages

John Harbour

Entrance is made from the green spar just south of Turtle Rock, marked by a beacon, at the western end of the Whalesback Channel. From this spar take a southerly course, pointing on the hill at the western end of Dewdney Island. When midway between LaSueur and Gowan Islands, swing gradually eastward so as to pass midway between the south-

AT ANCHOR IN CLEARY COVE

ern tip of Gowan and the Dewdney Island shore. Deep water carries through most of the harbor. The best anchorage is to be found at the eastern end, just east of the arm of land projecting northward from Dewdney. Note the rock off the northeast end of this arm and give it a wide berth before coming down into the anchorage, which carries fifteen feet over mud.

Dewdney Island has a varied terrain with good flat rocks for camping and swimming (as does the eastern end of Gowan), rock hills to climb, and woods to track through. John Island is much higher and steeper, but the slopes are easily negotiated for panoramic views of the North Channel. And John is crowned by a mature forest, where fascinating mushrooms abound after a rainy spell. If you're a trail-blazing hiker who brought your boots, you could hike for hours, or even days, among the ridges of John Island. The waters of John Harbour shelter pike and perch, and the surrounding shores are rich with blueberries in season.

For the shallow draft cruiser or small trailer boat there is a prized inner harbor, known as Cleary Cove. This bight in the north shore of Dewdney Island carries only four-foot depths at chart datum, but entrance is not difficult on either side of the largest island enclosing the cove. Once inside, the harbor presents a miniature Shangri-la seemingly shut off snugly from the world. It is a fine memorial to Edgar Dewdney, Minister of the Interior, later Lieutenant-Governor of British Columbia.

Moiles Harbour

Approach Bergeron Point through deep water in the Whalesback Channel. In high water years the point may look like an island. Entrance to the harbor is made between Bergeron and Aikens Islands. (How did a Quebec M.P. and the Lieutenant-Governor of Manitoba rate islands named for them here?) Note the rock off the northwest end of Aikens and approach the entrance from the northwest end of Bergeron, so as to avoid it. Then come down midway between the two islands into the harbor.

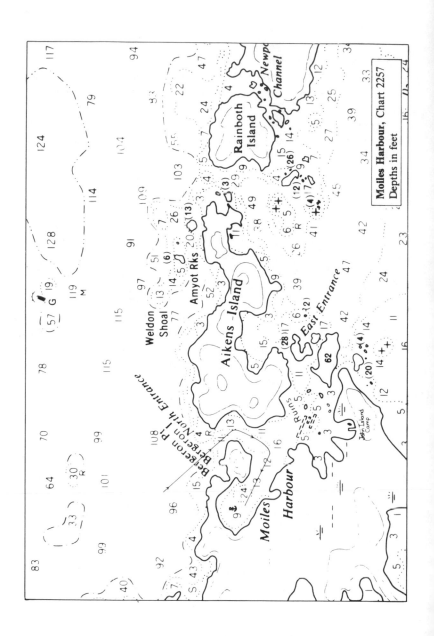

Molles Harbour, Chart 2257
Depths in feet

At the south end lie a few scattered ruins of the Moiles brothers' saw mill, but the village that grew up around it has disappeared. In its place stands the John Island Camp of the Sudbury YMCA. A hundred-odd children now frolic on the anomalous plain of sand, where some ancient seashore interrupted the rocky bluffs of John Island. The camp faces the "outer" North Channel, so only its small dock is visible from Moiles Harbour. This is a poor location in which to anchor, as the bottom is still foul with logs, sawdust, broken timbers, and all the debris of the old town site. It is also weedy and marshy. Drop your hook in the northwest corner of Moiles, where the holding should be better, but may be difficult at times, and where there are rocks to walk or camp upon, blueberries to pick, and a sunset to catch your breath.

The Whalesback Channel
Charts 2252, 2257, 2259, and 2268

If you are headed east out of John Harbour or west out of Moiles, wait, if you can, for a bright clear afternoon or morning. In either case, you have before you what is surely one of the most beautiful ten-mile passages in the world. The Whalesback Channel deserves the clearest atmosphere for display of its white and shaded rocks against the deep blue water, while dark pines march across the steep granite slopes or stand in bold relief against a limitless blue sky.

The Whalesback appears properly to begin at La France Rock on the western end (the *Sailng Directions* say Turnbull Island is the western terminus), but as you emerge from John Harbour you will pick it up at the green spar south of Turtle Rock. Keeping greens on the starboard hand and reds to port, the pilot must watch his buoys and keep count of his islands as he threads the track on the large-scale chart. Most of the channel is extremely deep, 60 to 100 feet, but it holds surprises for the vessel wandering off course. Even the shallow draft trailer boat must exercise care when out of the channel.

Meanwhile the crew can indulge in total absorption of the passing scene. The Whalesback Rock, which gives the passage its name, may not look much like a whale to you, but it seemed a mighty friendly leviathan to the surveying party sent out to sound the depths of the North Channel under Commander J.G. Boulton in the summer of 1887. The steamer *Edsall* carried three rowboats, each manned by two sailors. As one rowed back and forth across a section to be

THE WHALESBACK

sounded, the other swung the lead and noted his findings on graph paper. All day they were tortured as they worked by mosquitoes and blackflies, so Commander Boulton ordered camp headquarters to be made on the bare back of the whale. There would be fewer pests at night out on the naked rock in the channel than there were on the forested mainland. After a hard day's work the men gratefully beached their boats on the tail and climbed up to the head, 45 feet above the lake, for supper and a good night's sleep.

The narrowest part of the Whalesback is formed by John Island. So steep on the harbor side, from the channel the island looks almost pastoral, with its gently rolling fields of stone planted to a crop of moss and broken up by woodlots of pine and birch. Where John curves away to the south at Moiles Harbour, the channel widens and the eastern end becomes a large bay leading about eight miles to Spanish River. Along the north shore this wide part is named Aird Bay. There is a settlement on the open plain and an unloading apparatus for oil tankers—of little interest to the cruising boat crew or boat camper, although one might launch a small boat at Cutler, off Highway 17. But the north side of the narrow part of the Whalesback has some splendid anchorages.

Anchorages

Beardrop Harbour

Entrance can be made on either side of Turtle Rock. A course of 055° from the green spar on Colmer Ground will take you directly into the harbor, or you can follow a course of 012° from the green spar south of Turtle Rock until the center of the entrance comes abeam; then turn more easterly into the harbor. Holding is good anywhere under the massive bluffs on the south side of the anchorage in ten to fifteen feet over mud, but the best protection is obtained on the eastern side of the group of islands reaching out from the south shore. Keep the largest one close aboard on the starboard side as you come around, in order to avoid the group of islands and rocks standing out from the north side.

Lett Island

At the beacon on the islet just west of Nelles Island, turn out of the Whalesback Channel on a heading of about 013° for the western tip of Lett Island. (This seems to be the churchy part of the north shore; Reverend Samuel Sobieski Nelles was president of Victoria University in Coburg, and Lett Island was named for the widow of a Collingwood clergyman.) From the western end of Lett, a course of 341° will carry you right into the anchorage, offering woods and rocks for your enjoyment and a grandstand view of the Whalesback passage. Anchor in eight feet, sheltered from all winds save the rare southeaster.

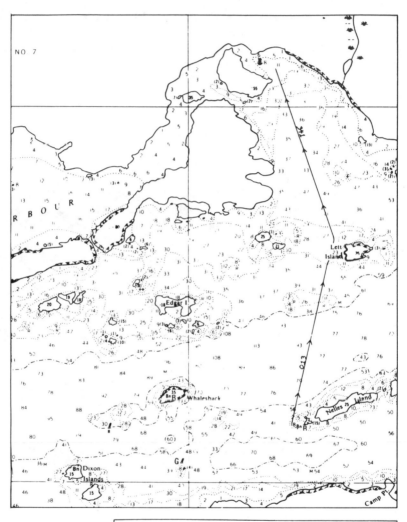

Lett Island Anchorage, Chart 2268
Depths in feet

The shallow draft boat can find passage and campsites between the outer entrance to Lett Island anchorage and Beardrop Harbour.

From Spanish to Little Detroit
Charts 2252, 2257, 2268

Where the Whalesback widens and approaches the Spanish River, the islands change in character; they become more thickly wooded, with fewer expanses of rocky outcrop. Now there's nothing intrinsically wrong with wooded islands, but somehow they aren't quite as interesting to look at as those which alternate forest and rock, they seem to be considerably buggier, and they aren't nearly as well suited to camping, picnicking, and hiking.

There is one cove and attractive group of islands on the north side, however, where overnight anchorage can be enjoyed by the cruising boat. Coursol Bay, on the southeast side of Aird Bay, and named for a Montreal M.P., is entered from the west in deep water past a magnificent cliff. Turning to port inside, shelter from all winds except south and southeast can be found under that cliff in ten feet. The far end of the bay, beyond the point, is foul and grassy, but is doubtless home to a large population of fish.

The islands, named from west to east, Brewerton, Thomas, Abigail, and Kirke, are all high and steep-to, and commemorate the first British capture of Quebec in 1629. Sir David Kirke commanded the expedition, which included officers Thomas Kirke, Captain Brewerton, and a ship named *Abigail*. Deep water passage into the bay they enclose can be had between any of them, but the best anchorage is in fifteen to twenty feet between Thomas and the seventy-foot high island just east of it.

As I noted earlier, the mouth of the Spanish River, including Frenchman Bay, is quite unexciting in this land of frequently breathtaking vistas. The south side of Whalesback Channel is formed here primarily by Aird Island and its satellites marching in line. Protected anchorage is available almost anywhere in this long, narrow bay; the most attractive spot is at the western end between Aird and Jackson Islands. Jackson was apparently a Georgian Bay inspector of fisheries, but who Lieutenant Bayfield had in mind when he named Aird Island and Bay remains a mystery.

If you're headed east from the Whalesback you will pass between Passage and Shanly Islands, marked by beacons and further enhanced by an arrow-minded vandal with a paint can. Slow down as you approach King Point. You are now at Little Detroit, the tightest passage on the North Channel. With government blasting and rock removal the channel is but 75 feet at its narrowest, although sixteen feet deep. The way through is clearly identified by beacon ranges and the pass is enlarged on chart 2268. From the west a course of 135° leads from the rear range on Green Island, and once in the pass, another rear ranged formed by Harrison Point light and the beacon east of it carries a course of 107°. Favor the mainland shore and you'll squeak through quickly. Little Detroit enjoys the saving grace of being short. Westbound helmsmen are blessed with front ranges on the opposite courses. Not only because it is narrow, but because there is a blind spot at the turn, mariners are required to broadcast a security call on VHF channel 16 before entering Little Detroit.

McBean Channel and Its Offshore Islands
Charts 2252 and 2257

Just around the corner from Little Detroit there is a deep indentation of the north shore, shaped rather like an upside-down boot. The toe of Shoepack Bay presents an imposing rock cliff as you round the point and come down into the harbor. It's hard to believe that just the other side of this splendid cove lies the comparatively pallid approach to Spanish River. If you would anchor here, however, you must carry plenty of line to drop your hook 25 to 40 feet down, or the mountain goats in the crew can leap ashore with long lines to tie off to trees while the boat nestles against the steep cliff face. The other alternative is to anchor in 15 to 25 feet in the heel of the boot, a less grandiose, but nevertheless lovely shore. Boat campers can enjoy several sites at either end, but the sole of the boot is a bit steep for camping.

As you cruise eastward in McBean Channel from Little Detroit, you have a guiding beacon in Mount McBean, a 620-foot peak. Although not the highest of the La Cloche Mountains, which begin here, it is one of the most readily identifiable hilltops on the North Channel, and certainly one of the handsomest. How ironic that this beautiful passage, its lofty terminal mountain, and the harbor at the foot of the slope should be named for a man described as "an ignorant, illiterate, common kind of fellow . . . .[he] has been a tolerable bruiser, and was at one time a tolerable snow-shoe walker." But the man who so described John McBean saw fit to place him in charge of the Lake Huron district of the Hudson's Bay Company for fifteen years, until McBean retired after 35 years in the fur trade. So perhaps he deserved these memorials to his name after all.

Approaches

If you are coming from the west and wish to anchor among the islands on the offshore side of McBean Channel, there are two ways to approach them: the slightly tricky way and the easy way. In the first case, on emerging from Little Detroit you will head southeast less than two miles for the green spar marking (M.P. and lumber king Alexander) Lumsden Rock. Leaving it to starboard, head east about nine-tenths of a mile until the unnamed island between Crooks and Hawkins (respectively, Ontario Minister of Education and Chief Justice) Islands is just abaft the beam in the opening. Then you will head for that unnamed island, watching your depth sounder carefully to avoid the shoal making out northeast from Crooks, and turning southeasterly again as soon as you have passed the hook on the west side of Hawkins. In these waters depths of 100 feet and 0 feet lie side by side. Once through the passage between Hawkins and its southwest neighbor you have a choice of two anchorages.

The easy approach to this island group is to continue down McBean Channel about five miles from Little Detroit to the green spar marking the shoal off Gillmor Point on Frechette Island. (an island memorial to a French Canadian poet with a point named for a New Brunswick M.P.). From there you simply follow the east side of Frechette Island around to the passage between it and Eagle. If you are coming from the east you will head more directly into the Frechette-Eagle passage from the red spar north of Fox Island.

Armour Island

An alluring hideaway can be found between little Armour Island and the northwest wing tip of big Eagle. A southerly course from about the middle of Hawkins' south shore will bring you to the north tip of Armour Island. Favor that shore, in eight feet of water, to avoid the rocky shoal making out from the tip of Eagle Island as you round into the harbor. Note the rock off the east shore of Armour. If the wind is blowing northwest through southwest, drop the hook in twelve to fifteen feet in such a way as to lie directly behind the island forming the southern shore of the harbor. That way you will avoid the surge that can come in when the wind is strong. This anchorage affords privacy and vistas, though only fair protection. Nor are there any really good campsites for the boat crew that sleeps ashore.

Eagle Island

If Armour is snug and tricky of entrance, Eagle Island harbor, a mile and a half around the corner, is open, easy, and, not surprisingly, less interesting. Just come on in. The only hazard lies over the rock shoal near the little island in the center. Favor one shore or the other as you enter and you'll be all right until you drop anchor in twelve to fourteen feet over clay. Eagle's shores are much like John Island's—alternating rock fields and woods, with many delightful campsites.

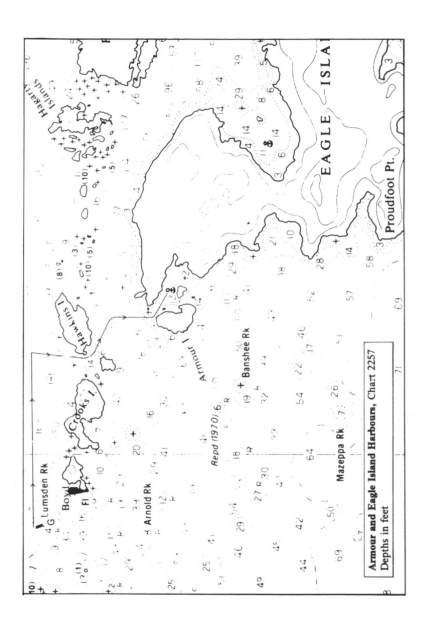

Armour and Eagle Island Harbours, Chart 2257
Depths in feet

Oak Bay
Charts 2252 and 2257

From the north tip of Frechette Island McBean Channel continues "officially" for another five miles. It remains a beautiful passage, but its most valuable secret lies through an inconspicuous opening on the north side. The North Channel comes in layers, and what has traditionally been called Oak Bay, an inside passage of an inside passage of an inside passage, is a whole cruising world of its own, with Mount McBean beckoning in the distance and a half dozen anchorages enticing you to linger close at hand. The newer editions of chart 2257 regrettably place the name only on the pool at the west end, while leaving the bay itself unnamed. Here we retain the name for the whole waterway. Hushed forest, rocky hills, placid lily pools, pike, bass, and blueberries all await your pleasure in Oak Bay. Let the wind and the seas rage outside—you can spend a week or a month here and find new nooks and crannies to explore.

Approach

Eastbound or westbound through McBean Channel, the approach is clear and the entrance the same. Three-quarters of a mile west of the green spar off Gillmor Point there is an opening between Graham Point and Hotham Island. Turn northward and come on in, right down the middle. Nothing complicated.

Anchorages

The closest beauty is at the west end of the bay between the bluff on the mainland—climb up for the view and munch blueberries on the way—and the stream that leads to the weed- and fish-filled pool now called Oak Bay on the chart. Anchor in ten feet over mud. Or you can drop your hook in the bight on the east side of the bluff in fifteen to twenty feet, but that spot might occasionally get an uncomfortable roll from the entrance.

Another choice lies to the right of the entrance at the west end of Hotham Island. Favor the north shore of that anchorage to avoid a four-foot shoal with some zero-foot rocks making out from the south bank. Anchor in about ten feet over mud.

As you move eastward in the bay, the first island you come to is known locally as Goat. It's a favorite camping place, although campers can find innumerable good locations all over the bay. As you cruise past the island, favor its southeast shore to avoid a rocky shoal in the middle of that passage.

The bight on the north shore, where the bay widens, does not provide good anchorage as the water is twenty to forty feet deep, where it is not barely covering rocks. But Perch Bay offers pleasant gunkholing for a dinghy, good fishing prospects, and camping sites. There are some cottages, however, at its entrance.

For the larger cruising boat Hotham Island (named for Lord of the Admiralty Sir Charles Frederick) provides the next two anchorages. To enter the westerly one, head due south from the eastern tip of the hook below the mouth of Perch Bay. Pass *between* the two little rocky islands shown off the eastern end of the Hotham Island peninsula enclosing the anchorage. Actually, the island closer to shore appears as two islands in high water years. The passage carries ten feet. Once past those islands, gradually swing westerly into the anchorage, favoring the north side somewhat, and drop anchor in ten to twelve feet. Perfect protection, paper birch mixed with the pine and oak, rock outcrop, reeds and lily pads, and a splendid view of Mount McBean are here for your pleasure.

The easterly Hotham Island anchorage is a bit more difficult of entry. As you move eastward through the deepest part of Oak Bay, you must have every single island to starboard identified. There are two that are somewhat larger than all the others. When, just beyond the eastern tip of the eastern one of those, you can see the eastern point of the anchorage entrance opening up, turn south to pass between that island and a group of smaller ones northeast of it. Head for the eastern side of the entrance. As you do, note the row of four little rocky islands off the west side of the entrance. The closest one is only three feet high, but must be identified so that you can pass between it and the eastern entrance point.

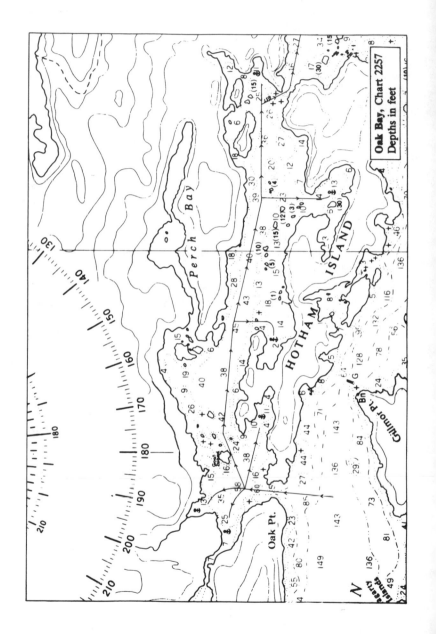

Oak Bay, Chart 2257
Depths in feet

Then continue down into the anchorage for good holding and complete protection in nine to twelve feet over clay. West of the little island in the anchorage, the bottom shoals sharply. There is one cottage at the foot of the cove.

The last anchorage in Oak Bay is as easy to get into as the first, but not as well protected if a strong west wind carries a chop down the length of the bay. Simply continue on the deep water course, favoring the north shore and keeping all the little rocky islands to starboard. Be alert for a two-foot patch just off the north shore north of the easternmost group of islets, but keep that spot to port. Head straight on to the bight in the eastern shore and anchor in twelve to fifteen feet over mud.

McBean Harbour
Charts 2252 and 2257

You have now run the three-mile length of Oak Bay, and when you are ready to leave you can exit by the same path you entered. Or, if a bit of the adventurous spirit burns in your soul, you can thread the eye of a needle and continue to bear down on Mount McBean on the inside passage. If you're ready for that, here is how it's done.

At the very eastern end of Oak Bay, where Hotham Island humps up and the mainland hooks down, there is a narrow passage (actually about 300 feet wide) with three rocks blocking it. But you can pass between them on a course of 158° from the eastern tip of the largest island just northwest of that passage. On that heading you will leave two of the rocks to starboard and one to port. When the middle of the pass is abeam, turn east and sail through it in 25 feet of water. It's really not complicated, it just takes care.

Now you can cruise on through for a mile and three-quarters to McBean Harbour. The only hazard is a group of rocks extending from the northwest corner of the unnamed island between Hotham and Lee, but it is easily avoided. The least depth of this passage is six feet off the northwest point of Lee Island. Alternatively, of course, you can enter the harbor the easy way, heading north from the beacon on Bald

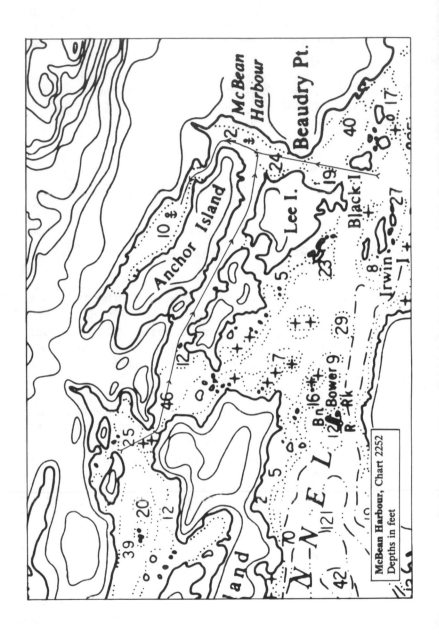

McBean Harbour, Chart 2252
Depths in feet

Rock in McBean Channel to pass between Lee Island and Beaudry Point.

At McBean Harbour you are as close to that mountain you've been chasing as you're ever going to get by water. In the outer harbor, where you can anchor in seven feet over mud, the woods recede from the shoreline and there are several cottages. When you pass through the channel leading to the long bay behind Anchor island—least depth of eight feet down the middle—you will find yourself back in the rock bluff wilderness once more. Anchor or camp where you will.

Note: The mainland shores of both Oak Bay and McBean Harbour are part of the Spanish River Indian Reserve. There are very few people in residence in this locality, but on occasion some of them have been less than friendly to visiting boats. It is best to anchor at a judicious distance from their homes.

The Benjamins and Their Neighbors
Charts 2252 and 2257

When the world was very young—a mere snippet in a small solar system—it seethed and boiled with the explosive energy of youth. The well-springs of that energy came from deep within Earth's core, and as it pulsated upward, it sought to escape the confines of its own skin. Sometimes that release was found, and the sparks flew high into the air above to cool quickly and settle down as rock. But often there was no way out, and great masses of molten magma could only spread out to solidify gradually in pools and veins beneath the heavy surface of hard rock enclosing them. Meanwhile, the pace of geologic time continued in unhurried measure. As it did, the forces of wind and rain and flowing water etched away the exposed surface, while the pushing kept on from below. Slowly, inexorably, the forces of erosion and uplift exposed bits and pieces, then great humps and slabs of trapped magma. And so were born the Benjamin Islands— startlingly pink as a brand new infant, though they now count their years at a couple of billion.

It seems especially appropriate that these most beautiful of North Channel islands bear the Christian name of a light-house keeper at Clapperton island. A stuffier tradition was maintained in naming Croker and its satellite, Secretary, after John Wilson Croker, Secretary to the Admiralty, 1809-30. The splendor of the Benjamin Islands and their largest neighbors, Fox and Croker, is well protected by a phalanx of encircling rocky shoals. But there is a safe way through for the watchful and the careful. In fact, scores of boats find their way every summer and the anchorages are often crowded.

Approach

Whether you are cruising to the islands from the west, the east, or the south, Fox Island Harbour is best approached from the McBean Channel side; entrance to the Benjamin-Croker group is made from the south side. For the latter islands, take the green spar southeast of East Rock at the east end of McBean Channel as your point of departure. Head southwest for a bit over three miles and pass Croker and Secretary Islands on the starboard side. You are now faced with a choice. You can either turn northwest just beyond Secretary Island to anchor in Croker Island harbor or at North Benjamin Island, or you can continue on through Main Passage (stay half a mile north of Robertson Rock light to clear the bad shoal it marks, or else pass between the light and the Clapperton Island shore) to enter South Benjamin harbor. Each anchorage is something special—you might want to try all three. If you are coming from southeast, the passage east of Clapperton Island is open; from the southwest hold well off Clapperton and its satellites until you reach Main Passage.

Anchorages

Fox Island

Locate the three islets on the shoal close to the northeast corner of Eagle Island. From the middle islet a course of 099°

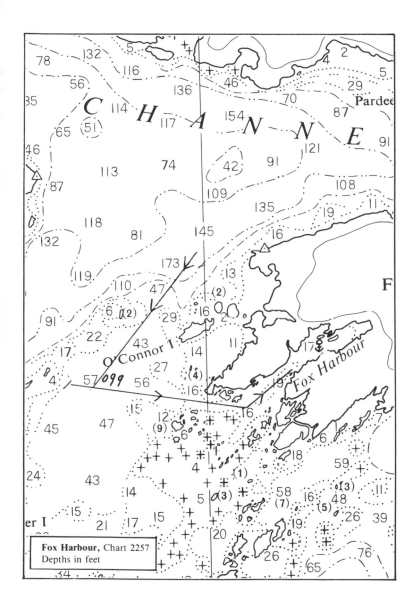

Fox Harbour, Chart 2257
Depths in feet

for about eight-tenths of a mile will lead you between two sets of rocks and islets off the west end of Fox Island. When the middle of the entrance to the long, narrow harbor is abeam, turn and move up its unobstructed center. While the course described carries depths of twelve feet or more through most of its length, there are a couple of spots with only three or four feet at chart datum. In a low water year entrance to this harbor might be risky for a deep draft boat.

Once inside, Fox offers several pink, smooth-faced coves to cozy up to and an archipelago of its own for dinghy exploration. A well-protected anchorage, it is free from the surge which is the price paid for the beauty of some of the other Benjamin harbors. There are some very small coves with expanses of open, flat rock that are ideal for boat camping and swimming. Green pine and blueberries complete the color scheme.

Croker Island

Enter from deep water on a northwesterly course, following the coast of Secretary Island at about 600 feet offshore, to avoid both the rock shoal making out from the southwest corner of the island and the patch of very bad water on the southwest side of the passage. Give Secretary a berth of about 800 feet as you round its northern end, to avoid its shoals and the rocks lying between it and the south side of the harbor entrance. Then head into the harbor at about 075°, keeping sharp lookout for the shoal extending from Porcupine Island.

The most sheltered anchorage is found under the high rock cliff at the south end, in twelve feet over mud. There is also good protection in five feet on the east side of the island at the bottom of the harbor, but don't attempt to pass around the south end of this little island. The northeast corner of the anchorage is another attractive spot, with a sand beach nearby, but it rolls a bit in southwest to west winds. The passage between Porcupine and Croker is too deep for anchorage and is subject to surge from the northwest anyway. The Croker shore is generally too steep or too thickly

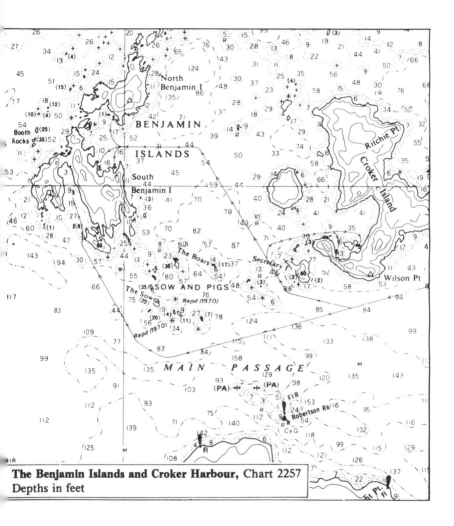

The Benjamin Islands and Croker Harbour, Chart 2257
Depths in feet

wooded for campsites, but there is good hiking along the top of the high south bluff. In fact, there is a well worn path leading from the southwest corner of the harbor, where much scraping of the earth has also molded a dinghy landing. The bass bite well in Croker harbor.

North Benjamin Island

Entrance is the same as for Croker. Just keep on going past Secretary for a mile and a half through good, deep water until the harbor between North and South Benjamin islands opens up on the port side. Then turn west and pass midway between the points of the two islands. There are two indentations of South Benjamin to choose from for anchorage in seven to eight feet, or you can cozy up to the southwest side of North Benjamin in five. Any of them offers good protection, but may be subject to some surge in east to southeast winds. All offer delightful rock climbing and swimming. There are a number of good tent sites in the harbor, although boat campers might prefer the less steep North Benjamin side. In low water years, that shore has a sparkling pink sand beach.

South Benjamin Island

South Benjamin harbor is perhaps the most spectacular of an impressive group of harbors. It is certainly the most popular, although you're not likely to find yourself alone in any of this group of anchorages, unless you beat or wait out the season. It is entered from the Main Passage north of Clapperton Island. There is little difficulty once the Sow and Pigs are unmistakably identified and kept well to starboard. The entrance to the harbor is centered by a rocky island six feet high. Despite the appearance of the chart, pass *between* that rock and the island southeast of it, favoring the island shore. There is 25 feet through that passage, but between the rock and the opposite point there are rocky shoals.

NATURE'S ROCK QUARRY, BENJAMIN ISLANDS

Anchor anywhere within the harbor in seven to fifteen feet over mud, except at the very end where the bottom shoals to three feet in weeds. There is a rock just off the eastern shore, about two-thirds of the way into the cove. Boat campers will do best tucked in behind the southeast entrance island. South Benjamin rolls uncomfortably in winds from the south, but that is about its only disadvantage. Fish, blueberries, magnificent vistas from its cliff tops, and delightful gunkholing in a dinghy among the other coves and passages of the island offer continuous entertainment. Look for the "quarried" blocks of stark white quartzite lying in a bowl of pink granite. Linger and enjoy. You have arrived at the glorious conclusion of the north channel of the North Channel.

~Five ~

Potpourri

The Big Islands
Charts 2252, 2257, and 2286

As you have passed openings in McBean Channel and come around to visit the Benjamins, you have seen a number of large islands lying midway between the north and south sides of the North Channel. They signify the startling change in geology and foliage between these two shores. In contrast to the pine-clad rock bluffs of the north shore, these islands are thickly covered with mixed forest and heavy underbrush. Nor do they offer, with one exception, especially interesting harbors. In fact, the most westerly two, Darch and Innis, provide none at all. Note that for most of the passages and harbors in this chapter you will be navigating on old-style chart 2286, with depths in fathoms and an additional correction needed for current chart datum.

Amedroz Island

Amedroz Island, six miles southeast of McBean Harbour, offers shelter on its north side under Bourinot Island. A clerk of the Admiralty is here protected by a clerk of the House of Commons. There is likely to be an uncomfortable surge from strong northwest to northeast winds. The approach is clear from all directions, but entrance is favored from the west side of Bourinot Island, to avoid the rocks found between its east side and (Librarian of Parliament) Todd Shoal.

Bedford Island

Six miles farther east there is another large harbor formed by Bedford Island, West Rous, and East Rous, all admirals. Again the approach is clear. Entrance is made between Macpherson Ledge and the Five Islands, favoring the latter. The west side of the harbor affords the best anchorage, in six feet over mud, with much better protection from high winds than Amedroz provides.

Clapperton Island

Clapperton Island, which honors only a naval lieutenant, presents two anchorages to the cruising boat. Logan Bay on the east side is easily identified by the flashing green light on the reef near its mouth. The approach is clear from every direction. Keeping the flashing green lighted buoy well to starboard, head due west into the harbor, staying at least fifty yards off Carling Point to avoid a submerged rock just north of it. Anchor in the southwest corner in six feet over sand. Appropriately named for an illustrious geologist, Sir William E. Logan, this cove offers protection from all winds except easterlies, which don't blow often, but when they do can give a steady roll here.

On the south side of Clapperton Island, Clapperton Harbour affords the best anchorage among the big islands in terms of both shelter and scenic interest. It is little Harbour Island that creates the protection, and on it is situated a sometimes resort with a tale to tell.

It began life in the late 1930s as a retreat for American executives. Inoperative during World War II, the place was transformed into Harbour Island Yacht and Fishing Club in 1949, when Harold Hutchings and his wife, Jamesie, set out to create a sophisticated haven for the daring yachtsmen who cruised the North Channel in those days of few charted soundings and fewer buoys. "Hutch" was a colorful man. He had owned and lost a bank, was involved in construction of the Alcan Highway, knew a great variety of people and charmed most of them, and he had danced at the Duke of Windsor's wedding. In order to create in the wilderness the kind of atmosphere he had in mind, he organized a club among his wealthy yachting friends to underwrite the financing of the resort, although the facilities were open to the public. Members enjoyed priority at the docks, however, and all charges were included in the annual dues.

For thirteen years Harbour Island Yacht Club was the pivotal rendezvous for families and friends cruising the North Channel. Only five boats called in the first year, but under the spell of Hutch's personality and good taste, membership reached over 2,000 in 1962. In that year an untimely death struck down Harold Hutchings. Jamesie made every effort to continue the operation during the next few years, but it was more than a woman alone could manage. Dues had been modest; one man of great wealth had borne most of the financial burden, and the white elephant in the woods became his by default. Benson Ford never occupied the place, however, and Harbor Island Yacht Club fell into disuse for five years, although boats continued to enjoy the anchorage.

Then, in 1970, it appeared that the charming old place would get a second chance after a new partnership bought it from Ford and restored it to operation. After a few seasons it faltered again, and for another period of years the buildings remained shuttered and the equipment idle. In 1979 yet a third revived and renovated Harbour Island Yachting, Fishing, and Hunting Resort opened its doors. Now it, too, appears to have staggered under the difficulties inherent in running a rustic resort on a somewhat remote island in a somewhat remote body of water. When you get there the attractive main lodge building, with outlying guest cabins, may be boarded up or open and welcoming, docks may be in place or pulled up on shore, the dining room and bar may be serving nightly or the place utterly deserted. These days there's always a bit of suspense as you come around the island from the channel to see what, if anything, is happening at the club. But whatever the status of the shore facilities, Harbour Island still affords sheltered and pleasant anchorage in twelve feet, from opposite the buildings almost to the Clapperton Island shore.

To reach the harbor from east or west, or from the north via the east side of Clapperton Island, you must transit the narrow, though well-buoyed, Clapperton Channel. The red- and white-striped daymark, topped by a flashing red light, on Meredith Rock identifies the entrance course to the green spar off Beverly Island. (Beverly isn't a girl—it's Sir John Beverly Robinson, a lieutenant-governor of Ontario.) Keep well clear of the shoal making out from Burbidge Island, which sometimes uncovers. Beverly is also equipped with a red- and white-striped daymark, flashing white. From the spar follow the deep bay around the coast of Harbour Island to the anchorage. Clapperton, like all its neighbors, was thoroughly logged early in the century and the bottom still conceals many logs above the sand, so your anchor may not grab on the first try.

Solomon Point to Eastern Island
Chart 2286

The first Solomon to arrive in this part of the world was a young German Jew who came out to trade kettles and rum for furs in 1762. He was one of the first three "English" traders to reach Michilimackinac after the conquest from the French. As such, he was doubly a pioneer, for the northwest Indians hated the English and he nearly lost his scalp to the allies of Chief Pontiac in 1763. But he didn't, and as a result there have always been numerous Solomons populating the upper Great Lakes.

If, before turning south through the Benjamins and Clapperton, you cruise eastward along the north shore past the point bearing this family name, you, too, will be something of a pioneer. Well, perhaps not a pioneer, but certainly an adventurer. For north of the offshore chain of islands no hydrographic soundings have been published, and such shoreline and island contours as are shown on chart 2286 derive from the drawings Lieutenant Bayfield made 150 years ago. If there burns in you a little of the explorer's fire, you will want to learn something of what lies there. The best way to do this, if you enter in a cruising boat, is to anchor it firmly in one of the locations described below, and explore the roughly eight by one and one-half mile cruising ground by dinghy. If your vessel is already a shallow draft boat you can choose almost any of the islands on which to make camp, as only a very few are inhabited. In either case, exercise the usual precautions of slow speed and lookout with polaroid sunglasses. In these unsounded waters rocks with one inch of water over them pop up from forty-foot depths.

The rewards will be worth the effort. The islands display great variety in size, shape, and forest adornment, all backed by the ridged heights of the La Cloche Mountains—so close, now, that you feel certain a few steps ashore would bring you to their steep bases. As so often happens with mountains, though, they are farther from shore than they look. To climb to a summit you would have to slosh through a good deal of swampy underbrush close to shore and between the stark, rock ridges. If you have a sturdy pair of hiking boots and a land compass, go to it.

An easier way to indulge a desire to hike, and at the same time treat yourself to some of the loveliest sights along the North Channel, is to bring your small boat into the stream marked Fort La Cloche F.S. on the chart. Those canny old Scots fur traders knew how to pick a spot on which to settle and lure the local Indians with the miracles of English industry and distillery art. By the side of a placid stream, where the soil is deep enough to grow crops and fodder for the post occupants and their livestock, Fort La Cloche was built by the Hudson's Bay Company in 1821. From here John McBean managed the whole Lake Huron district until he retired in 1837. But by the 1870s the trade had declined beyond the point of profit in maintaining the station. Today only a crumbling chimney made of limestone blocks remains above ground to mark the old fort, although archaeologists have uncovered some building foundations.

The site of old Fort La Cloche has had several reincarnations since the Hudson's Bay Company closed it—first as a sawmill and later as a tourist camp, most recently as a Ministry of Natural Resources Junior Ranger camp for 24 girls aged 17. They maintain the camp buildings and grounds—a house, three cabins, a dining hall, a small dock, and a playing field. It is the base from which they work on provincial parks in the area. A road connects the camp with Massey, a dozen miles away.

The camp authorities are hospitable to visitors, and there is a concrete launch ramp here from which a trailer boat can explore this section of the North Channel. What Fort La Cloche has most to offer, however, is a series of sparkling waterfalls cascading at quarter-mile intervals from Lake La Cloche to the pool at the old fort site and the short stream that empties into the North Channel. Bring your small boat into the "river"

FALLS OF THE LA CLOCHE RIVER

mouth between the weed beds along the shore, move up a quarter of a mile, and tie to a tree along the left-hand bank below the first waterfall. You can stop for lunch at one of the picnic tables on the lane leading to the camp.

In back of the house next to the falls is a flight of steps. At the top you will enter the world of Hansel and Gretel—a forest path deep and soft with pine duff and cloaked in shade from the tall hemlock, birch, and pine. But this forest is rarely hushed. One or another of the waterfalls is always audible as you follow the path a mile or so to Lake La Cloche, and each of the falls is more impressive than the last. Other trails and old logging roads fan out from the riverside to show you through the woods and over the high outcrops of precambrian rock.

Anchorages

Given the limitations of chart 2286, only three anchorages are readily accessible.

McTavish Island

McTavish Island, named for a Hudson's Bay factor—at Fort La Cloche, of course—is marked on the south side by a red spar a couple of miles east of the beacons at the end of McBean Channel. After passing that spar (be sure to locate it if approaching from the east or south), head for the southeast point of McTavish. Rounding that point, pass midway between McTavish and the island immediately northeast in a minimum depth of seven feet. Take care to skirt the shoal extending from the north point of the eastern end of McTavish, then anchor in the shallow cove of the island's north side in sixteen feet of water. The shingle-beached and thickly wooded island is fairly deep-to. Protection from northwest through northeast winds is rather minimal at McTavish, although it is a scenic spot and easy to get into.

Matheson Island

Matheson Island anchorage, one and one-half miles east of McTavish, and named for a mere boatman on the survey steamer *Bayfield*, offers quieter lying. A course of about 084° from the southeast tip of McTavish Island will bring you through very deep water to the two rocky islets off the

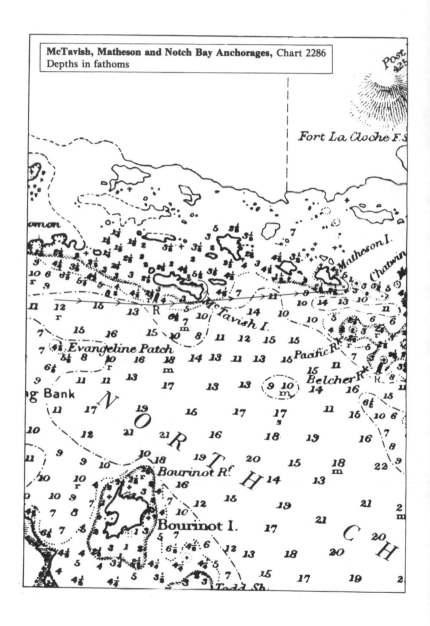

McTavish, Matheson and Notch Bay Anchorages, Chart 2286
Depths in fathoms

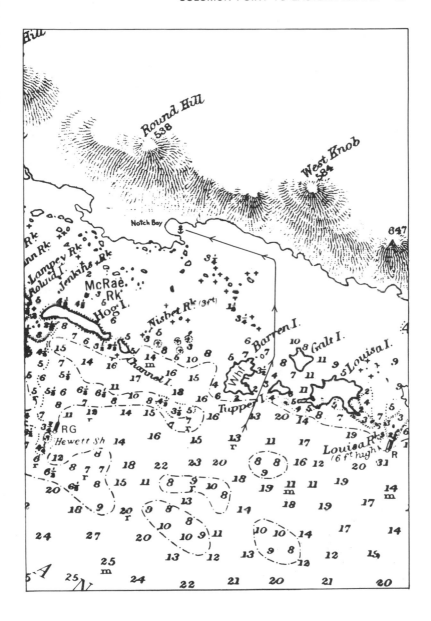

southeast point of Matheson. Keep those islets fairly close aboard the port side to avoid a rock, sometimes submerged, to the northeast. You should carry no less than twelve feet as you round to the north side of Matheson and into the wedge-shaped anchorage between it and the long island north of it. The outlines of the latter are incorrectly shown on chart 2286. Anchor in twelve to twenty feet, protected from all westerly winds, but open to northeast through southeast. Matheson Island is the anchorage closest to Fort La Cloche if you plan to go over by dinghy.

Notch Bay

Three miles farther east is the entrance to the third anchorage. It must be approached from offshore. If coming from the west, leave the red spar marking Belcher Rock to port; if approaching from the east, the red spar off Louisa rocks (she was Commander Boulton's wife) must be left to starboard. Locate Barren and Tupper Islands and pass midway between them. Head almost due north across the bay to the notch in the mainland hills. Your course should carry a minimum of twelve feet, but will be mostly forty to fifty feet deep. Turn west and coast the mainland, 75 to 100 yards off, into the bay just west of the notch.

Most of the bay is shallow, with depths of two to four feet, but in the center it drops off rather sharply to an arc of 20 to 25 feet. The best spot to lie is just inside the southeast point, where you can place your anchor in fifteen to twenty feet at the drop-off. This is a rather restless harbor with a surge in winds from northeast to south. On the south side of the harbor there are rocks for climbing and cookouts, and on the south side of the peninsula forming the bay is a sand beach.

The anchorages described for cruising yachts are rather heavily wooded for boat camping. But there are numerous other islands in this archipelago that do have good campsites and which are accessible, with care, to shallow draft small boats.

Bay of Islands
Chart 2286

From the peaks of the La Cloche Mountains an extended finger of rocky ridge thrusts southward into the North Channel about twenty miles east of McBean Channel. In so doing, the La Cloche Peninsula creates two bays: McGregor on the east and Bay of Islands on the west. Each is a potpourri of islands—hundreds of them in all shapes and sizes. These islands are, in reality, lesser mountain peaks like those of the mainland, for between them the water lies very deep. How deep is but scantily revealed on chart 2286 for Bay of Islands, and for McGregor Bay chart 2245 shows nothing beyond the entrance. Both bays were discovered long ago by the cottager. He first came with the railroad back at the time of World War I, and has been coming ever since. As a Johnny come lately in this part of the North Channel, the cruising yacht and its crew must accept conditions as they find them or stay out.

With respect to Bay of Islands, the latter alternative may be the wiser until a larger scale chart is issued with more detailed soundings. For those who insist upon exploring here, however, there are a few scattered buoys along the main channels. Cruising sailboats must be especially cautious. While many of the formerly hazardous overhead power lines have been buried in underwater cables, some remain to menace a high mast. Shallow draft trailered boats and outboard dinghies can poke around the roughly eight- by three-mile bay with far less danger to propellers and keels, but even they must exercise caution. Proceed slowly, keep a lookout, and use a depth finder if you have one. The speedsters one sees darting around are local cottagers, for the most part, who know where the rocks are, and even they occasionally come to grief.

Although not hospitable to cruising yachts, Bay of Islands is one of those areas that is more suitable to canoeing than other parts of the Channel. Because of the sizeable cottage population, secluded camping locations are not as readily found here as elsewhere, and campers are not likely to be welcomed enthusiastically if they park themselves too close to a cottage.

The La Cloche Peninsula forms the east side of the Bay of Islands and provides access by highway to launching sites. Great La Cloche Island creates the southern enclosure—a low, alternately wooded or swampy island that is something of a topographical and geological misfit in the North Channel. It is entirely owned by one man, who carefully sustains the local wildlife. Between these two landforms and the mainland shore lies the obvious explanation for the bay's name. Not all of the islands are inhabited by any means; the northwest part of the bay, farthest from the highway, is the least populated.

Approach

Bay of Islands can be entered only from the west. Its north shore can be approached directly from the Solomon Point to Eastern Island area, discussed in the last section. East of the Louisa Rocks, however, there is no buoyage and few soundings to guide you. Cruising boats should enter the bay along its south side, where there are some anchorages easily accessible to them. From the west the approach is quite clear. From the south along Wabuno Channel, give Halfway Island and the islets around it a good berth before turning east to enter the bay.

Great La Cloche Island Anchorages

Bell Cove and Sturgeon Cove indent the Great La Cloche shore side by side about two miles into the Bay of Islands. Bell Cove is easy to enter from the east side of Neptune Island, down the middle of the entrance, but most of it is quite deep for anchoring. Given the rocks off Neptune Island and the point opposite it at the cove entrance, the best spots to lie are under the middle of Neptune Island (but watch carefully for the shoal extending from the east end of the islet south of this spot) or along the southwest shore below the two little islands south of Neptune.

Sturgeon Cove is equipped with a beacon range (not shown on chart 2286) to guide you in at about 138° with a minimum depth of six feet in the channel. Notice the rocky shoals off Alert Point and stay carefully on range until past them. This cove is about ten feet deep throughout, so you can anchor anywhere. Both coves suffer surge in northerly winds; both are thickly wooded to the water's edge.

Boat campers will find more suitable and more scenic sites along the north shore of the Bay of Islands, and among the islands themselves there are some uninhabited places to choose from.

To reach an exceptional place by small boat or dinghy, follow the north shore of Great La Cloche Island until the deep indentation of La Cloche Channel opens to starboard. Proceed south for three and a quarter miles to the bottom of that channel, past the old sawmill on the port shore. This large bay is very deep throughout, but a cruising boat can find 10-foot depths for anchorage near the mill. There are also several cottages in this area, but you aren't here for the atmosphere of La Cloche Channel itself. Launch your dinghy, or continue on in your small boat, around the bend to port. Duck your head as you pass through the viaduct and keep a firm hand on the tiller. This tiny pass is called Swift Current, although the turbulence known here by the old voyageurs has been forever stilled by the causeway built overhead to carry the trains and automobiles of advanced civilization. Beach your boat on the port shore, just beyond the viaduct, and walk a few steps down the dusty road to read the historical marker.

As you pass through the viaduct and continue on your way, you will find yourself transported to a place of startling contrast to the tepid shores of La Cloche Island. You have entered a gem of a waterway, and the central stone in the setting is the 220-foot high cap of Dreamer's Rock. Legend says that the Ottawa youths who lived here long ago selected that isolated peak for the seven-day solitary fast during which an initiate adolescent learned of his destiny in dreams and hallucinations. Surely if any place has that power, this majestic hill surrounded by its own reflection in the peaceful water would be so endowed. You, too, may give yourself over to daydreams as you circle around the peninsula.

At the south end of the bay, on the west shore of the gut between Great and Little La Cloche Islands, are the bell rocks that have given name to these islands and their backdrop mountains. You might want to land your boat to look for them and even send a message as the Indians did long ago. From here the small boat can pass into McGregor Bay, the twin to Bay of Islands on the other side of La Cloche.

As you round Dreamer's Rock you will see a lodge on the peninsula shore. Birch Island Lodge is an American plan resort, accessible only by water, but only a half mile from its parking lot off route 6 near Swift Current.

Birch Island Landing

Near the northern entrance to La Cloche Channel is Birch Island Landing, essentially a series of parking lots for the Bay of Islands cottagers and guests of The Island Lodge, an American plan resort in the bay. Most of La Cloche Peninsula is part of the Whitefish River Indian Reserve, and the Birch Island Band operates a small boat marina mainly for local boats. If you walk up the road you will pass the community center and a cluster of houses. At the highway one of Birch Island's proud moments in history is recorded in bronze. Franklin Delano Roosevelt, avid fisherman that he was, spent ten peaceful days angling in the waters of the North Channel, en route to the Quebec Conference of August 1943. Across the road can be seen the parking lots and small boat docks for the cottagers of McGregor Bay. If your outboard needs gas, it can be obtained here.

Whitefish Falls

Nestled into the northeast corner of the Bay of Islands, the village of Whitefish Falls lies along the Whitefish River. Its widely unrecognized claim to fame is that the first Ontario nickel was discovered nearby, even before the vast deposits at Sudbury were found. As a resort community, Whitefish Falls began to develop in the 1930s under the nurture of an enterprising partnership consisting of two couples called Stump and Spry. They began Holiday Lodge in 1935, established the general store, and operated a grocery boat service that brought dockside shopping to the cottagers in the Bay of Islands. A flashing white light atop a black, white and green square daymark identifies the river entrance, where least depth is four feet.

Dockage and Marine Services

A quarter of a mile below the village, on the starboard side, is a small government dock with five feet of water alongside. There is a launching ramp, but no other facilities. The cottage resorts on either side of the river do not cater to transient boats, but they might sell gas. Forbes Holiday Resort, on the west bank, might have room at their docks in twelve-foot depths. They provide gas, ice, water, electricity, heads and showers.

Whitefish Falls, about fifteen miles from Trans-Canada 17, is a convenient point of departure for the trailer boat or boat camper to cruise Bay of Islands and the Benjamins. Les' general store in town presents a good selection of edibles, and Whitefish Falls Tavern serves meals. The major entertainments here are fishing and swimming. A ride of a mile or so upriver from the government dock will bring you to the falls.

McGregor Bay
Charts 2245, 2286, and Defoe Map

If you came to the North Channel by way of Lake Huron, the Bruce Peninsula, and Tobermory, you passed the place where the clan McGregor was planted in this part of North America. Captain Alexander McGregor was fishing and fur trading out of Goderich, Ontario—in fact, doing anything to turn a shilling—in the early 1830s. In the course of his coastal wanderings he fell upon the Fishing Islands near the northwest tip of the Bruce. His fortune was made in this fabulous fishing hole, and he contracted with a Detroit firm to supply 3,000 barrels of fish a year at one dollar per barrel—big money in those days. He enjoyed the distinction of building the first European structure on the peninsula, a stone shelter for his hired men on Main Station Island. But more enduringly, he founded a dynasty on the North Channel, and his progeny would rise to positions of leadership among the descendants of his wife's people.

Son Duncan worked for the Hudson's Bay Company at Fort La Cloche in the mid-nineteenth century, and grandson George was elected chief of the Birch Island Indians during the World War I period. Great grandson, William McGregor, served as chief of the Whitefish River Reserve for over forty years until he died in 1967, followed by a fifth generation McGregor to preside over the band. This bay, which is the playground of happy holiday makers from two nations, perpetuates in its name the blending of two proud races on North American soil. But long before that it was the resort of Indians, whose remains lay secret beneath the soil of Old Birch Island, now called Wardrope. In the 1940s archaeology dated the graves at 300 years or more. McGregor Bay has been beloved of men for a long time.

Like its sister, Bay of Islands, it is a province largely of the cottager. No marine chart shows its hundreds of islands in accurate detail, nor its treacherous depths which may vacillate between sixty feet and six inches within a boat length. 2245 and 2286 are virtually useless once you are much past McGregor Point. But there is a map that shows a few approximate courses. If you dare, you can attempt to thread your cruising boat through the myriad islands along the tenuous lines shown on this quite accurate scale drawing, known as the Defoe Map, obtainable at Turner's in Little Current. Harry J. Defoe, an accomplished navigator, began cruising the North Channel in the late 1920s. He compiled the map from several Canadian government maps, private aerial surveys, and the advice of friends who owned cottages in the bay. He then had one of the expert draftsmen in his engineering department commit the diverse sources to a single, scale drawing. The first edition rolled off the print-making press of Defoe's famous shipbuilding company at Bay City, Michigan, in 1935, with new editions published in 1948 and 1966.

There are still a few overhead power lines in McGregor Bay, but most are buried, so that the cottagers may enjoy an uncluttered sky over their bay. Nevertheless, my advice for cruising yachts, both sail and power, is the same for this bay as for Bay of Islands: enjoy similar splendid scenery elsewhere. To the shallow draft trailer boat or dinghy, and even the canoe, I say come on in, but be careful.

Approach

There is only one deep water entrance to McGregor Bay and it must be approached from the four-mile expanse of Frazer Bay to the south. Pass between the red and green lighted buoys off McGregor Point. The beacon on the steep-to point can be taken fairly close aboard. Then turn northeast to keep all the little islands at the entrance to McGregor Bay on your port side. About one and one quarter miles past the beacon you can take either a northerly course at midday or early afternoon or an easterly course in the afternoon. From there you're on your own and the Defoe Map. No word description of the courses would be of much help. Proceed dead slow, keep your depth finder sounding, and place the polaroid sunglasses on the nose of the lookout on the bow. That advice goes for shallow draft runabouts as well as deep draft cruisers.

Dockage and Marine Services

There are no docks for overnight lying, but Turners' McGregor Bay has dockage for boats transacting business at their general store, which is the commercial hub of the bay. It is located on Iroquois Island, near the northwest corner of the bay, at the place marked "Post Office" on the Defoe Map. In addition to postal service, Turners' provides gas, groceries, liquor, ice, bait, and repairs for small boats.

Sharing Iroquois Island is an institution of quite a different cast. St. Christopher's Church, a simple structure of knotty pine, whose 12 steps were carved from the island's granite, satisfies the spiritual appetites of the bay's cottagers. Although built in 1951, its origins go back to 1910, when Stuart

Jenkins of Toronto was one of the first to homestead Crown land in the bay. At age 65 his doctor told him to find a more salubrious climate than Toronto, or die. Whether or not it was the air of McGregor Bay that preserved him to age ninety, he set aside land for a church on his island. Several Jenkinses were more or less buried on that section—their coffins were laid down on the bare rock, then covered with concrete—and when government regulations did away with private cemeteries the family decided the time had come to convert theirs to a churchyard. And so was born St. Christopher's, for summer worship by reportedly overflow crowds in shorts and running shoes.

Anchorages

At the entrance to McGregor Bay you can follow the range toward the scenically intrusive Canada Cement Mill, then turn the corner of Little La Cloche Island to enter the "Boat Passage" that leads to Dreamer's Peninsula. The controlling depth is seven feet, but the entrance is narrow where a four-foot shoal makes out from the northwest shore. Once inside, anchorage can be found under the impressive peninsula, although the terrain on the south shore of this bay is flat and weedy.

Some years back the McGregor Bay Association set aside a special anchorage deep in the bay for cruising boats, in order to preserve the mutual privacy of both cottagers and yachtsmen. It is virtually the only part of McGregor Bay that is undeveloped. Lying about eight and a half miles from McGregor Point, the Anchorage, as it is known, is situated north and east of East Sampson Island. Boat campers may, in addition to this location, find isolated spots on a number of the islands in the bay. As in the Bay of Islands, they should take care not to park on the doorstep of a local resident.

~Six ~

Close to the Mountains

Departing Harbour Island or the Benjamins, less than twenty miles of cruising will bring you to what appears to be the end of the North Channel. Don't be deceived. New delights await you beyond the quarter-mile narrows of Little Current. The north shore dips down only momentarily, via the anomaly of Great La Cloche Island, to touch—almost—the northernmost tip of Manitoulin Island. But the two do not meet, and the "little" current often flows swiftly to keep them apart. All ships and their crews who would traverse the North Channel must pass this strait. And so, like the Bosporus, an urban center has grown up here. For the moment we won't stop, but will go on to the very end of the Channel and then return to stay a while.

Frazer Bay
Charts 2205 and 2245

At Little Current you leave the soft blue La Cloche Mountains behind you and approach a more remarkable range, the Killarney Mountains. Technically part of the La Cloche range, the Killarney group is really distinctive enough in appearance to warrant a separate name. For devotees of the Rockies or the Alps, or even the Appalachians, calling the uplifts that back up the North Channel mountains may seem like a poor joke. But heights, like most other things, are relative. Furthermore, if these peaks seem lowly, it is only because they are worn down by the burdens of age—almost two and a half billion years. They were formed from some of the oldest rocks known to man and were ancient long before the Rockies and the Alps were born.

You will get much closer to the Killarney Mountains than you could to the La Cloche because they send their foothills right down to the North Channel in long fingers of tall bluff. These extensions of the tantalizing peaks on the horizon, which seem to be covered with patches of snow among the dark pines, can actually be climbed from their water-lapped bases. And then you discover that what makes them glisten in the sun is not snow but almost pure white quartzite.

Approach

Your first approach is across Frazer Bay, entered at a red spar a little less than five miles from Little Current. Enfolded by two arms of pine-clad quartzite, the bay is deep and clear almost throughout. It is a wedge-shaped body of water, and a strong west wind can pile up quite a sea at the narrow eastern end. Oddly, the origin of its name has been lost.

Anchorages

There are several coves on the south shore of Frazer Bay, but most of them are open to northwest through northeast across the wide fetch of the bay, and therefore roll uncomfortably when the wind blows from those directions.

Boyle Cove, closest to the entrance, is open and rather deep for anchorage, but there is a good campsite on the western side not far from the entrance. Boyle was only a draftsman for the Admiralty and probably never saw his namesake.

Near the eastern end of the bay there are two coves under the island at the northern terminus of Rat Portage. The island is known as Blueberry, although unnamed on the charts. The best protection is found in the eastern cove right up under the island, in twelve to fourteen feet of water. There is a cottage on the Blueberry shore, however, and courtesy would dictate that you not anchor there when the owners are in residence. Most of the western cove is very deep, in addition to being somewhat exposed to northwest winds, but in the southeast corner you can find depths of twelve to sixteen feet. When anchoring here sailors must be careful of an overhead power line that is ostensibly on land, but hangs partially over the water. There are good campsites in both coves, as well as blueberries, of course, and the scenic views are as impressive as any to be found in this country of visual delights. Scale any of the white cliffs around you for a gull's eye view. Beach the dinghy at the outlet of the Rat Portage and follow a voyageur's woodland trail to the placid lake in the middle of the ridge and beyond to Portage Cove in Lansdowne Channel.

The extreme eastern end of Frazer Bay offers a more bucolic, but well-protected, anchorage. The entrance is crossed by a power line 33 feet high; the narrows into the

ALONG THE RAT PORTAGE

cove carries no more than five feet. Here the scene is totally different. The quartzite peaks are hidden from view by deciduous trees, and the bay is thick with reed patches.

Baie Fine
Charts 2205 and 2245

There are several places on this continent that lay claim to being "the only true fjord in North America." The prestige of singular authenticity notwithstanding, Baie Fine comes close enough to being a fjord to satisfy my convenience for description. In a word, it is magnificent. But it carries the most abused name in the North Channel. To my knowledge, there is no Irish tradition in this vicinity (Killarney is another story), so why the mellifluous French Baie Fine should have been so pervasively corrupted to Bay Finn (and even Bay of Finn) I am at a loss to understand. For years the Canadian Hydrographic Service avoided the problem by referring to it as Narrow Bay; then, for a while even they succumbed to Bay Finn. Now, at last, the charts and *Sailing Directions* have restored the old spelling. It is to be hoped that visitors will also be reconditioned.

Approach

Baie Fine opens from the north side of Frazer Bay and lies between the two fingers of quartzite bluff that form the north shore of Frazer Bay and the south shore of McGregor Bay, Killarney Ridge and Blue Ridge, respectively. The approach is clear and well marked. As you pass the narrow, almost hidden entrance at Frazer Point, follow the buoys and the track on chart 2205 very carefully for the nine-mile passage to the end of the bay. At the eastern end favor the north shore, leaving all the islands to starboard until the last little group before the narrows, which should be left to port before you make the turn. Here, as elsewhere, there are sudden and potentially catastrophic changes in depth. Identify each island as you pass, look around when you're in the clear, and enjoy. Caution: in low water years a five-foot spot in mid-channel at the narrows before the last passage to The Pool will limit the draft to be safely carried through.

Dockage and Marine Services

But you may want to postpone your passage to the end of the bay for a while. Okeechobee Lodge, long a favorite stopover for cruising boats, is open again after several years of shuttered solitude. Situated right on the point, the lodge's dining room overlooks the expanse of Frazer Bay, while its marina is sheltered in Baie Fine. Finger docks for alongside tieup in six to ten feet, gas, water, ice, heads, showers, and laundromat complete the marine amenities, while the lodge's lounge, bar, and billiard room are also open to boaters. If you haven't been doing too well with rod and reel on your own, there are fishing guides with boats and motors here to show you where to find the big ones.

Anchorages

Mary Ann Cove

There are numerous indentations along the shores of Baie Fine that invite a stopover at anchor. Some are quite deep, but the bay is so well protected that most are comfortable, although a strong, direct west wind can rile up the sea even in here. One of the popular anchorages is Mary Ann Cove, on the south side about two miles beyond the lodge, unnamed on the chart. Enter from the west side of the island, anchoring behind it in about twenty feet over mud. There is a nice campsite on the west shore. If you climb the bluff on the south side, you might find a plaque placed there many years ago by a grieving widow in memory of the husband with whom she shared a cottage on the island.

Directly opposite, on the north side of Baie Fine, is another cove, but it makes a poor anchorage because of its great depth of forty feet over rocks. From the head of this cove, however, there is an old portage to McGregor Bay and a trail to the top of the hill with a magnificent view for reward. Anchor in Mary Ann and dinghy over.

The Pool

One of the boating fraternity's favorite anchorages in the North Channel and, therefore, one of the most crowded in season, lies at the end of Baie Fine. Called The Pool, it is like a mountain lake, still and reflective in its total isolation from all winds. The bottom is mud and weeds, twelve to twenty feet down; sometimes it's hard to get a good anchor hold through the soft stuff. There are some good campsites at The Pool, but with many of the visiting boats tying off to trees against the rocks, campers may have to jockey for position. But campers do have a choice of islands all along the fjord on the way down, as there are only a few cottages located here.

When you passed into the narrowest part of Baie Fine, you entered Killarney Provincial Park. From The Pool there are trails that lead to Cave Lake from the southeast corner and to Artist Lake from the northeast side. On the latter you will cross one of the blazed park trails, which you can then follow for some serious hiking. Remember, this is rugged country. Wear proper boots and carry appropriate hiking equipment. It is also canoe country. One of the trails you cross is actually a portage within the canoe route system of the North Georgian Bay Recreational Reserve (see Appendix D for information sources). And if, on a first visit, the scenery seems reminiscent, it is because this country was portrayed for the world by the famous Canadian Group of Seven painters. A number of the lakes are named for them, and the cottage on a rock at the entrance to The Pool was a sometime summer home to them.

Lansdowne Channel
Charts 2205 and 2245

Outstretched fingers of the Killarney foothills enclose not only Frazer Bay, Baie Fine, and McGregor Bay, but reach in one more riband to the southwest, creating Lansdowne

Channel between Frazer Bay and the open waters of Georgian Bay. Yes, this is the boundary, the last stretch of the North Channel, beyond which lies an altogether different body of water surrounded by a different kind of terrain. And it provides a fitting eastern climax in its passage between the high bluffs, unnamed save for the Lion which sleeps atop with his Head and Rump sticking up. There are rocks beneath the water of this passage that honors no less a personage than the fifth Marquis of Lansdowne, a governor-general of Canada. They are far down in some places, close to the surface in others. But the channel is well buoyed through its nine-mile length from Frazer Bay to Killarney and, with reasonable care, offers no trouble.

If you're the sort who looks for adventure in a big boat, or you'e cruising in a small one, you might want to enter or leave Lansdowne Channel through Hole in the Wall. This is the name given to the slender passage, eight feet wide at its tightest, between (naval officer) Creak Island, marked by a lighted daymark, and (physician-fur trader) Badgeley Point. Don't attempt the passage in a strong west wind, which may set you onto the rocks at the narrow ends. Keep about twenty yards off the Creak Island shore to the point of the island, and then hug the Badgeley Point shore through the narrows until you fairly enter Lansdowne. You should carry no less than seven feet in low water. The whole distance is less than half a mile.

The beauty of Lansdowne Channel is rudely interrupted near its eastern terminus, where the north shore has been eaten away in huge chunks by the hungry jaws of a giant steam shovel, now at work on consumption of Badgeley Island as well. For over seventy years the Indusmin Killarney Quarries have found the world in need of the rich silica that underlies the pine and the blueberries, and Killarney men are well satisfied to find steady employment so close to home. Once past the mine, you're back in the primitive majesty of the land under the mountains as Killarney Bay opens before you.

Anchorages

Browning Cove

Geographically, Heywood Island is not on the Lansdowne Channel, but topographically it is a logical extension and lies only two miles west of the channel entrance. Nobody knows who Bayfield had in mind when he named Heywood, but Browning Island, in the bight of Heywood's north shore, honors an officer in the British Survey Service and creates an appealing anchorage. From east or west note the green spar marking Shoal Island Spit and keep well clear of it. The entrance to Browning Cove won't show up until you are due north of it. When it does, simply turn south and enter to the west of Browning Island, keeping midway between the island and the Heywood shore.

There are a number of anchoring sites to choose from in Browning Cove. The west end offers good protection in twelve feet over mud. Swing wide of the shoal making out from the southeast corner of Stanley Point as you come in. The anchorage at the foot of the cove, in fifteen feet over mud, may be subject to rolling when the wind blows strong from northwest through northeast. The passage south of Browning Island is ten to twelve feet deep, clear of obstruction, and offers a picturesque third alternative. But there is sufficient swinging room for only a couple of boats before it widens into the eastern anchorage, which gets a bit weedy in the southeast corner.

The shores of Browning Cove are forested almost to the water, but east of Browning Island there are a number of rocky islets with some woods that make excellent campsites for the small boat. Watch for rocks and shoals north of the southern boundary of Browning Island, however. On the west shore of Browning Island there is an open, rocky patch, good for camping, on which someone once painstakingly constructed a low table and benches out of stone. Dine there in style.

Snug Harbour

The name suits it exactly. Unless you're looking for it, you wouldn't know this deep, quiet haven exists on the north side of Lansdowne, just opposite the opening between Centre and Badgeley Islands. This is the widest part of the channel, deep and clear. When the most easterly tip of Centre Island is abeam, as you follow the buoyed course, turn northward and the entrance to the harbor will open up as you approach. Don't turn until you are in line with the eastern tip of Centre, as there are four- and five-foot patches in mid-channel west of that point. Favor the west shore as you enter the anchorage, and you should carry eight feet through the passage. Once inside, the water is deep and you may have to proceed almost to the end before you can drop your hook in 25 feet over mud. The shores are mostly wooded, but there is a tiny beach at the end from which a trail leads to an inland lake.

Killarney and Its Bay
Charts 2205 and 2245

It's been riding up ahead of the bow for quite a while now, this ultimate destination that gives its name to the pink granite and the mountains that have loomed before you—Killarney—the North Channel extremity that is both an ending and a beginning. And so it must have seemed to Etiènne Augustin Robert de la Morandière; only it wasn't Killarney then.

De la Morandière had wandered all over the Great Lakes and turned his hand to many things. He had traded with the Indians for fur, he had fought with the British at Fort Mackinac in 1814, and he had kept store for the garrison and small settlement on Drummond Island. Now something inside of him harked back to his ancestors on the estate of D'Estreche in France and his boyhood home of Varennes in Quebec. At 53 years of age he wanted to settle on the land and create a permanent home for his growing family. It wasn't a very good site for farming, and why he chose it remained a secret that died with him. But settle he did, on the beautiful strait known then by the Mississagi name of Shebaonaning—Place of the Long, Narrow Passage. Back into the bush from the rocky waterfront, he and his sons felled the trees, built a home and outbuildings, planted crops, brought in cattle, and founded a dynasty in the first permanent white village on the shores of the North Channel and Georgian Bay. The year was 1820.

Etiènne and his family were not the first to settle the

awe-inspiring land under the mountains—not by 9,000 years. Old Doc Greenman made that discovery during the twenty years that he and his University of Michigan graduate students dug in the hills back of town. They extracted layer after layer of man's remains until they came to the oldest of these, revealing where an ancient race had lived on a lakefront beach. Now that site is almost 300 feet above the water.

Their work and their good times here finished, Doc and his kids left behind them a monument in addition to the advancement of knowledge and endearment in the hearts of Killarney people. They left two cabins on John de la Morandière's farm. One of them was endowed with a monumental fireplace and chimney, built by the camp cook out of rocks his fellow students collected by hand. In return for his labors, Charlie was permitted to reside in the cabin the following winter to write his poetry undisturbed. Only the stone chimney remains on the site, still straight and tall. The cabins have been removed to the waterfront residence of the present owner of the land to serve, respectively, as a mother-in-law cottage and a sauna.

And what of Etiènne de la Morandière's farm? It supported a family of six sons and four daughters. As the children grew and married, and a few other families came to settle the farm became a village. But how did Shebaonaning, a village populated by Frenchmen, become "Killarney"?

As early as 1846 there was a post office with the official name of Shebaonaning, Upper Canada. Then, so one explanation goes, the town had the misfortune to host, for a few fleeting moments, an illustrious guest. In 1854 this unremembered government official was passing through by steamer on an inspection of the remote portions of Upper Canada. The charming settlement on the red rocks under the white mountains somehow reminded him of his native Killarney. When he returned to Toronto, he had the temerity to ordain the name officially changed; he, himself, never returned to learn how the residents felt about it.

Though the establishment of Killarney was inspired by farming, its future and its fortune lay seaward. Not surprisingly, agriculture never really took hold, and by mid-century Killarney men were netting and shipping in great quantity the silver wealth that lay beneath the waves of Georgian Bay. Their communication with the rest of the world was entirely dependent upon the schooners, steamers, tugs, and water craft of all descriptions that plied among the towns now rapidly growing up on Georgian Bay and the North Channel. As roads were built and the railroad cut through the forest, Killarney, at the tip of its 42-mile long, narrow peninsula, remained isolated by land. Though its citizens prospered from fishing and its sons found lucrative work in the silica quarries on Lansdowne Channel and the logging camps and sawmills of Collins Inlet, the town was cut off from the automobile that changed the face of North America. Thus Killarney was "preserved" as a seaside village until 1962, when Ontario Highway 637 was finally built for the sole purpose of linking one village to the major north-south Route 69. Now Killarney teenagers enjoy the privilege of being bussed 65 miles each way to high school in Sudbury.

The automobile has not spoiled Killarney, not yet at least. The village population hovers at about the same 450 to 500 it has been for several generations. No new commercial building to speak of has occurred, except for a small addition to the eighty-year-old Sportsman's Inn. The summer cottage population has grown, but it is primarily island- and water-oriented. The atmosphere remains gently old fashioned—unhurried, unpretentious, and hospitable.

When you reach Killarney you have reached the turning point in your North Channel odyssey. It is the place that finally and indisputably divides the waters of the North Channel from those of Georgian Bay. But be not dismayed; it is not necessarily an ending. Though you may here exit to climb back into your car or to head south through Georgian Bay or to the east shore of Lake Huron, you may, alternatively, turn around and retrace the North Channel on its opposite shore. And for those who have just come north it is only a beginning; they have all the North Channel before them. Here, then, is not a terminus, but a place of meeting, of coming and going. So it has been for voyagers ever since the first brigades of birch bark canoes transited the strait that led them from the sheltered North Channel to the French River-Ottawa-St. Lawrence route to the fur-greedy white man at Quebec.

You may wish to linger in Killarney before you turn elsewhere. It is a place of startling color contrasts, where the red and pink rocks rise boldly from the depths to meet the heights of white quartzite, where the dark pines murmur their comfort to both, where the perch congregate in masses in Killarney Bay, and where trails can be found for getting back into the rugged interior.

Approach

Boats coming north from Lake Huron proper usually stop over in Tobermory at the tip of the Bruce Peninsula before jumping off for Killarney, about 50 miles across the northwest corner of Georgian Bay. If weather changes, or the distance is too far for a slow boat, you can break up the passage at anchor in Club Island harbor or Rattlesnake Harbour on Fitzwilliam Island, both a little less than half way. From southern Georgian Bay ports of origin, boats may follow the inside Small Craft Route northward or make longer passages in the open bay. In any case, the final approach is guided by Killarney East Light, a square white lighthouse that stands out against the red rock on which it sits, and is equipped with fog horn and radio beacon.

If approaching from Lansdowne Channel, simply follow the buoys and the lights by a necessarily circuitous route into the harbor.

Dockage and Marine Services

Killarney is a magnet for cruising boats, and there are several choices for dockage, all of which are likely to be crowded by late afternoon during the height of the season. Each is described here in sequence from west to east. All but one are on the north side of the strait. All have sufficient depth for deep draft sailboats.

A and R Marina offers dockage along three faces of an aging, L-shaped pier; gasoline, water, electricity, block ice, head and shower are available.

Sportsman's Inn is a modernized turn-of-the-century hotel with a newer motel annex and extensive dockage on both sides of Killarney Channel. Marine services include gas, diesel, ice, water, electricity, pumpout, heads, showers, and laundry (open to the public). The dockmaster monitors channel 68. For the crew there is a lively bar, patronized as well by local people, and a dining room where three meals are served.

The government wharf near the liquor store is of the usual sturdy type with no services. Most of the front face is reserved for the Indusmin silica quarry boat, which ferries men and supplies back and forth at each shift change, and all the children in town swim from the beach at the inner end. In between are several wood docks for local and visiting boats. The launching ramp for trailer boats is also located here.

GOVERNMENT DOCK, KILLARNEY

On the south side of the channel opposite the village, the George Islanders is a friendly marina operated informally by Tom and Ann Ken. Their house, perched on the hillside, looks like it originated in Grimm's Fairy Tales. Actually it was Killarney's first schoolhouse, circa 1840, which they have restored. They offer alongside tieup at floating docks in five to twelve feet, electricity, water, pumpout, heads, showers, outdoor tables and chairs from which to enjoy the view, and pickings from their vegetable garden.

Killarney Mountain Lodge is a handsome resort at the east end of town. It was built by the Fruehauf Trailer Corporation in 1946 for customer entertainment. For some twelve years a steady parade of visitors enjoyed luxury in the wilderness accessible only by yacht or the fleet of company aircraft maintained for the purpose. When Chairman of the Board Roy Fruehauf ran into trouble over his questionable dealings with the Teamster's Union's James Hoffa and with the Internal Revenue Service, he lost his exalted position and the company moved to divest itself of the extravagant white elephant that had been his brainchild.

In 1962 the property was bought by present owners Maury and Annabelle East, who have fashioned an American plan resort that graciously combines creature comfort with informality, and caters to both land- and water-based guests. Except for a couple of new buildings, the property looks much as Fruehauf left it, including the landing ramp for the ten-passenger, twin-engine amphibious plane, and the colorful flower beds laid out by the talented Dutch gardener.

Floating docks, gas, diesel, water, ice, electricity, propane, and pumpout are all provided for visiting boats; channel 68 is monitored for reservations. The crews are invited to use the facilities of the lodge, including the swimming pool, sun deck, children's playground, shuffleboard court, tennis court, sauna, showers, cocktail lounge with music, dining room, and evening entertainment such as movies and (toy) horse racing.

Killarney has been a fishing town for 150 years and, by virtue of its isolation, its fishermen are skilled at engine mechanics and hull repair. Indeed, some of them have built pleasure boats on order. Repair services are available from several individuals, who also have marine railways. Matti Salmela is a high rigger also trained as a machinist and welder, and is knowledgeable in electronics. Inquire of the dockmaster where you stop if you have need of any of these services. Although the facilities are not fancy, the quality of workmanship will probably be superior. If you need repairs to self or crew, there is a health center in town, staffed by an emergency nurse; a doctor comes in from Sudbury once a week. There is also an ambulance and helicopter pad for evacuating serious cases.

Activities for the Crew

As a village Killarney has more to offer than its rustic and unpretentious main street reveals at a glance. In the food department, Pitfield's General Store, with the old Jackman name board still in place, is the most impressive building in town, except for the church. A handsome example of nineteenth-century frontier commercial architecture, its interior retains the antique atmosphere with a high tin ceiling and massive oak counter. Even the old post office wicket still stands hidden in a corner. Be not deceived by the store's old fashioned look, however. It carries a modern line of quality groceries and meats. There is even a dock on the waterfront side, should you wish to shop by boat, and you can buy your gas or diesel here, too. If you're on foot, the store will deliver a large order wherever you are docked.

A few steps up Channel Street from Pitfield's, the characteristic white and green freight shed at the government dock has been converted to a fish market, supplied by Killarney's own tugs. Outside the store fish 'n' chips is dispensed from the Mr. Perch lunch wagon. Where the highway (Charles Street) meets Channel Street Parkside Grocery also has a full line of food products. Walk a couple of blocks up the highway from Channel Street to find a house just the waterfront side of the Bell Telephone Company building, with a side street intervening. (These detailed directions are necessary because there is no sign on the house.) Here you can buy delicious fresh bread and whatever else the proprietress has found time to bake that day. Liquor, as noted earlier, is dispensed at a store next to the government dock. If you want to sample another meal out, Rock House Inn serves lunches and dinners. One additional store, The Quarterdeck, sells imported and Canadian gifts, souvenirs, and a few books.

In addition to eating, Killarney offers several choices for recreation. You can visit the Centennial Museum on Commissioner Street, one block up from Channel, to learn more of Killarney's history, or find the original de la Morandière home on the west end of town. If scuba diving is your hobby, the Dive Shop at Sportsman's Inn supplies equipment and boats for exploring a variety of wrecks round about. Two of them were locally built tugs, the *Wilma Ann* and the *M.J. Low*, both 65 feet and scuttled in deep waters when they outlived their usefulness. There is also the "underwater parking lot", three cars and three trucks, all standing upright on the sand bottom.

Finally, if you like to hike, Killarney presents one of the best opportunities on the North Channel. There are a number of old logging roads and trails emanating from Highway 637 as you follow it out of town. Nearer to hand, Ontario Street will bring you, after a mile or so, to the lighthouse on Red Rock Point. If you are staying at Killarney Mountain Lodge, ask for the map of its walking trail, blazed through fields and woods back of the lodge.

Six miles from town lies the entrance to Killarney Provincial Park, a vast wilderness area of lake chains and mountain ranges devoted to the backpacker and canoeist. (There remains one campground for motorized campers, at George Lake near the park entrance.) There are also several trails suitable for day hiking. Transportation to the park can be arranged through Sportsman's or Killarney Mountain Lodge. Should you want to do some distance hiking and camping or canoeing, Killarney Outfitters, near the park, can supply all your equipment needs.

Anchorage

There is little place to anchor in the busy, narrow waterway that fronts the village, but hidden in Killarney Bay is one of the most dazzling anchorages in a land of many breath-takers. Portage Couvert is a shimmering pool, entirely enfolded in towering, pine-studded bluffs of snow white quartzite. So secluded is it that unless the water level is very high you cannot see its entrance until you are there. Seclusion does not mean solitude, unfortunately, for Portage Couvert (translated into English on the chart) is one of the most popular anchorages on the North Channel. But even if you must share with a number of other boats, it is big enough and of sufficient splendor to make that sacrifice worthwhile.

From Killarney I prefer the course east of Sheep Island, although that is not pecked out on chart 2205. Keep Sheep

PORTAGE COUVERT

island fairly close on your port side as you round it. From the tip of the island off to starboard that carries the electric lines, a course of about 325° will point you in the direction of a mass of black rock on the northwest shore of Killarney Bay. When you are about 100 yards off the northwest shore, you will see the entrance to Portage Couvert open to port. Turn and head for the south side of the entrance, in order to avoid the long, rocky shoal from the north point which all but closes it up. When you are past the narrow entrance, turn immediately north again to avoid a small shoal extending from the south side. Then anchor anywhere in this absolutely quiet refuge, in seven to nine feet over mud.

The cove itself doesn't have very good camping sites, but just outside on the south shore are some level rocks and woods. The rock climb from the western end of the cove will give you, across the half-mile portage, a panoramic view of Frazer Bay and its eastern anchorage that you may have enjoyed a few days before.

~Seven ~

The Home of Gitchie Manitou

The North Channel is many places and many moods, but everywhere along its length one senses an ineffable presence. Through each opening among the islands and across every expanse of open water there, brooding on the horizon, are the silent, majestic bluffs of Gitchie Manitou's great island—sometimes light and ghostly in the fog or blue haze of a summer morning, sometimes softly green and reassuring in the brightness of sunlight, sometimes heavy and dark as storm clouds congregate above the heights. Is the benevolent spirit himself whispering to you of the mystery of life? The ancient Ottawas believed this. It was here, their sages told them, that Gitchie Manitou gave to the Ottawa people the secrets of the growing of maize from seed—a gift of life whose presentation was immortalized for the white man by a new England poet, when he sang of how Hiawatha wrestled with the youth Mondamin.

The spell of Manitoulin, cast by the awe-inspiring parade of cliffs and headlands, is greatest from offshore. As you approach the giant island, the houses and farms and the prosaic furnishings of man show you a gentler, more comfortable and familiar face of the spirit. Manitoulin has always expressed this duality. The Ottawas of old venerated the island as the holy dwelling of the Manitou, sent by the Master of Life to bring them His blessings, but they farmed it and made it the center of their village life, as well. And the white man has continued the tradition. The Isle of the Ottawas, Odwa-minis, is still a place of farms and villages.

Despite its celestial protection, Manitoulin has not always known peace and prosperity. In 1648 the first white man, Father Joseph-Antoine Poncet, wintered among the Ottawas there, to show them the way of the Frenchman's God. But within two years the fury of the Iroquois descended on the island, at the same time that it destroyed the homeland of the Hurons along the southern shores of Georgian Bay. The two tribes fled together to the comparative safety of Lake Superior. Then toward the close of the century, when the French had brought the Iroquois under more effective control, some of the Ottawas came drifting back to their ancient home. A strange trouble awaited them, however, and by 1700 the island was virtually deserted. Had Gitchi Manitou lost his power? Was he engaged in a long battle against the evil spirit, Motchie Manitou, so that the crops would not grow while they wrestled, and the game and the fish fled too? Or did a fire, set by the people to drive out evil spirits, escape control and ravage the entire island? No one has yet found the answer to the mystery. It is known only that the island was shunned for some 125 years.

Not until a lieutenant-governor of Upper Canada decided that the Indians should be encouraged to settle down and farm on reserves set aside for them did the Ottawas return in any numbers. They were joined by Ojibways and Mississagis and Saugeens, for the government scheme would see all the Indians of Upper Canada conveniently located in one place, leaving the rest of the province available for the enjoyment of British settlers. It didn't work, of course. The Indian nations never did assemble en masse in any one location. And, in time, the whites came to covet Manitoulin along with the rest.

The settlers tamed the island in the traditional ways of all frontiers: they cut down the forests, farmed the land, and fished the waters. Their descendants are still doing it. There are fewer farms than there once were (cattle and hay are the chief "crops"), such forest as is left goes to only a handful of pulpwood companies, and the commercial fishing is mostly ended, but the way of Manitoulin life is not greatly changed beyond the stringing of roads and power lines. Not so far. The latest breed of settlers may do more to alter the island than anyone before. The year-round population of about 12,000, including 5,000 Indians, grows to 35,000 in summer. In some places summer cottages sprout like mushrooms, while many of the farms are bought by city folk hankering after the land. Development hasn't reached epidemic proportions yet, so there is still much remote roaming to enjoy, both by land and by water. But camping on whatever rock strikes your fancy is not feasible here, as it was on the north shore or the east end of the North Channel. On Manitoulin, the car or boat camper must sign up for a spot in one of the numerous organized campgrounds.

Manitoulin Island has an impossible shape. Its northern coast consists almost entirely of a series of long, wide bays indenting the high, wooded bluffs, and sometimes penetrating almost to the south coast. The piloting is easier here than elsewhere on the Channel. Deep water, fewer hazards, and more aids to navigation enable your lookout to rest in the cockpit most of the time. Because the bays are generally clear of obstructions and lie in a north-south direction, while breezes prevail from southwest to northwest, each of them affords good sailing. The south shore also has one of these bays, but otherwise it presents a smoothly sloping, boulder-strewn beach to the onslaughts of Lake Huron. In addition, Manitoulin is studded inland with four large lakes and 104 smaller ones. It would seem that this largest freshwater island in the world is barely land at all.

Wikwemikong
Chart 2245

Care to "go foreign," though you never leave Canadian waters? Then head southwest out of Killarney for the independency of Wikwemikong. Wikwemikong, where the beaver were once plentiful enough to give the place its name, is where the Ottawas first resettled on their return to Manitoulin in the second quarter of the nineteenth century. In 1832 a Catholic mission was established under Father Proulx—the first church on the North Channel. The land on top of the high bluffs was fertile and the settlement flourished and grew, while elsewhere on the Manitoulin Reserve the grandiose government scheme to settle all the Indians of Upper Canada never really got off the ground.

By mid-century white settlers from the older counties between Georgian Bay and Lake Ontario were clamoring for access to Manitoulin. In 1860 the Indians held a big council at West Bay and agreed to a united resistance to cession of their island. As a result, the first government attempt to negotiate a treaty ended in stalemate in 1861. Were the Indians learning some bitter lessons at last? No matter. In 1862 the government sent a better persuader. William McDougall, Superintendent-general of Indian Affairs, upped the ante from the 50 acres per family offered the year before to 100 acres to every family head, plus lesser amounts to each child. And the money paid by white settlers for their land would be put into a trust fund (after deducting the costs of the survey and expenses of the Indian Department, of course) for the benefit of all the tribesmen. This was a tempting offer to many of the chiefs assembled at the council at Manitowaning, although the men from Wikwemikong were not deceived. In fact, one threatened to knife any of their number who signed the treaty.

Saturday's negotiations ended in deadlock once more, and while the council recessed over the sabbath, the Wikwemikong band returned home across the bay. By Monday morning McDougall had sweetened the offer some more, and when the Wikwemikong group arrived back on the scene, the superintendent's tactic of divide and conquer had succeeded. He had approached every man individually to obtain the necessary signatures. The Wikwemikong band was infuriated to the point that three of their own members who had capitulated were ostracized from the community. With their priest in the lead, these proud men stalked back to their land, and to this very day Wikwemikong remains the only unceded Indian reserve in all of North America.

And a goodly piece of land it is, consisting of the whole 250-square-mile east end of Manitoulin Island. The couple of thousand people who live there seem to reflect the pride of their nominal independence, although, in fact, they participate in all the government programs designed for their more conciliatory brethren. Many of their farms are prosperous, and substantial numbers of the villagers work off the reserve. Nor is the Wikwemikong band neglecting the potential of the tourist trade. The first weekend in August the annual Pow-Wow attracts crowds from far and wide to watch (and in the case of Indians from the Canadian West and the U.S., to participate in) the pageants and dances, eat traditional Indian food, buy skillfully executed handicrafts, play games, and dance the night away to square, round, and rock music.

Approach

Wikwemikong village is perched on the bluff looking east over Smith Bay. The spire of Holy Cross Church stands as a beacon to the sailor coming home from the sea, but shallows at the base of the bluff limit that sailor's draft to three feet. A cruise of about sixteen miles across the top of Georgian Bay from the eastern exit of Killarney Channel will bring you to the government dock. You want to keep clear of the mess of rocks and shoals extending south and west from Big Burnt Island, but the flashing red lighted buoy at Campbell Rock gives you a guidepost to avoid trouble. From there, a course of 258° will just enable you to avoid Goldhunter Rock off Cape Smith.

Dock

The government dock at Wikwemikong is T-shaped, with a long extension from shore. Dockage along the extension is suitable only for very small boats; it also serves as a jumping-off place for the swarms of children swimming there on a summer day. Cruisers should moor at the outer end. There is no suitable anchorage here, as the bay is wide open to east and north. Nor are there any facilities, although minimal groceries are available in the village. One docks at Wikwemikong to enjoy the hike up the bluff, to visit the graceful church and its historic graveyard, to look with sorrow at the gutted stone shell of the boys' school next door—destroyed by fire during the winter of 1954, when snowdrifts on the white man's part of the road prevented the fire trucks from getting through—to attend the Pow-Wow, or to walk in the countryside.

South Baymouth

The tourists who come to Manitoulin and the North Channel by car from the south arrive first at the south coast indentation, logically called South Bay. *Chi-Cheemaun*, the Big Canoe that carries 140 cars four times a day in summer from Tobermory, docks at the village terminus of that bay, also logically named South Baymouth—with emphasis on the last syllable. If you want to linger a while at this hamlet, populated by a number of summer cottagers, there are three motels: Wigwam, Buck Horn, and Huron Motor Lodge. The Wigwam has a restaurant and the Family Brown Restaurant is a quarter of a mile away on Highway 6. There are a couple of gift shops and the Northern Crafts Gallery, featuring Canadian, especially Manitoulin, crafts, in association with the Manitoulin Pottery School. The 1898 Little Red Schoolhouse is a charming village museum. A couple of miles out of town the Ministry of Natural Resources Fisheries Research Station, where biologists developed the delicious splake, a cross between speckled and lake trout, is open to visitors. South Bay offers expansive protected waters for fishing and small boat sailing, with some good camping sites, especially on its wild eastern shore.

Manitowaning
Chart 2286

To reach the North Channel from South Baymouth you must drive about twenty miles north on Route 6 to the village of

Manitowaning. A few miles before you get there, Black Rock Resort on South Bay combines the American plan with trailer parking. In town accommodations are available at Hembruff's Motel and Wayside Motel, and Wayside has a restaurant. For a more luxurious land-based vacation, Manitowaning Lodge offers excellent food, attractive cottage rooms, exquisite flower beds, swimming pool with sundeck, shuffleboard, and children's playground. In addition, rental boats and motors are available, or you can launch your own boat to explore Manitowaning Bay and the east end of the North Channel cruising grounds.

Manitowaning Bay, the second from the east end of Manitoulin Island is typical of all the others. Sheltered by high hills on either side, wooded with the dark pine and light birch of the north country, the sea rolls gently here, except during a gale from the north. It was quiet on a balmy day in May of 1882, when the propeller *Manitoulin* made her way toward the village of Manitowaning, a regular port of call between Collingwood and Sault Ste. Marie. The passengers were enjoying a hearty lunch in the dining salon, only four miles from their destination, when the signal that strikes terror into every person at sea penetrated the air—fire! But the fortunate *Manitoulin* was commanded by "Black Pete" Campbell, who would become legendary in these parts for his resourceful, if unconventional, methods. Calmly he sent orders to Mate Playter on the bridge to turn the ship and run her up on the nearest beach, then warned his frightened passengers to remain quietly on deck until escorted ashore by the ship's crew.

The blaze was still confined to the engine room, and the crew executed the captain's orders smoothly and efficiently. The chief engineer remained at his fiery post to hold open the throttle that would give the ship full speed toward shore, lifeboats were swung out to be at the ready, and a young deckhand quietly jettisoned the 500 pounds of blasting powder carried on deck for consignment to the Canadian Pacific Railway. Most of the passengers cooperated with Captain Campbell and awaited further instructions. Eleven jumped in panic from the burning ship. Yet it took only six minutes from the first terrifying signal until the keel of the vessel bumped and scraped on the pebble beach. The lifeboats weren't even needed; every passenger waded ashore, Captain Pete bringing up the rear with a child in his arms. They reached safety none too soon, however, for by that time the ship was enveloped in flames and would burn to the water line. When all were assembled a census was taken. As the roll call was completed, the entire company realized with horror that eleven people had not answered. All of those who, in their frenzy, had cast themselves into the lake failed to reach the shore.

Ironically, Manitowaning, believed to be the precise location of Gitchie Manitou's dwelling, was the scene of the first white settlement on Manitoulin Island. When the lieutenant-governor of Upper Canada conceived the notion of solving the Indian problem by settling them all on Manitoulin, he never intended merely to move them in and then leave them to their own devices. They must have education and the blessings of Christianity, and to this end an official Establishment was set up at the foot of Manitowaning Bay. Captain T.G. Anderson, Indian Agent, moved his headquarters here from Penetanguishene; Reverend C.C. Brough established the Church of England; Dr. Paul Darling ministered to the health of the community; and Reverend Benjamin Bayly taught school.

These four men, with their wives, children, servants, and a few artisans—34 people in all—set out from Penetang in an open boat on October 10, 1838, while their possessions and provisions rode comfortably in a proper ship. Storms immediately broke over their unsheltered heads. For three cold, wet, turbulent weeks they struggled up Georgian Bay and around the headlands of Manitoulin to their destination. Finally sighting the village on October 30, the miserable party thankfully stepped ashore only to discover the mission house that had been built for them lying in a heap of still smoldering logs. With it had burned most of their goods, provisions, and medicines, stored there many days before from the schooner. Fortunately, the superintendent's house and the school remained intact, and all 34 people crowded into these two small structures. The schooner was supposed to call one more time before winter set in to leave additional provisions, but she never arrived and the pioneer party passed a grim winter in short supply. As happened on so many other frontiers, the youngest members of the party, the Bayly infant and one Darling child, did not survive.

But the Establishment was begun, and each year additions and improvements were made in the facilities—sawmill, smithy, carpentry shop, store—as the number of Indian families slowly increased. The annual "giving of presents," which were actually installment payments in merchandise for the purchase of ceded Indian lands, was transferred to Manitowaning from Amherstberg on Lake Erie. At the peak of attendance in the 1840s, as many as 6,000 Indians congregated from all over the Great Lakes in order to receive the allotments of blankets, cloth, needles, and knives carefully specified for each man, woman, and child. For a few days the bluff bustled with crowds and teepees and campfires, until the British government declared it would no longer bestow its largesse on Indians known to reside on the United States side of the lakes. (The U.S. government had given up these large assemblages some years before, in order to avoid the infiltration of Canadian Indians.) Thereafter the attendance diminished drastically.

The permanent Indian village built by government artisans was never as large or successful, however, as the rival Catholic mission across the bay at Wikwemikong, which was constructed by the Indians themselves. Many bands preferred to settle at other places along the North Channel, such as Birch Island, Sagamuk near Fort La Cloche, and Whitefish Falls. Nevertheless, St. Paul's Church was built in 1845, a simple yet graceful structure that remains to this day an active house of worship—the oldest in northern Ontario. The community limped along until the Treaty of 1862 opened the island to the white settlement that gradually transformed Manitowaning into a farm market center and a shipping port for logs and pulpwood.

The way was smoothed for conclusion of that treaty by one of the most colorful personages in local history. Chief Assiginack, Black Bird, an orator of great renown and a government interpreter for many years, was probably responsible for the success of the negotiations, despite the opposition of the Wikwemikong band and his advanced age, reportedly 94. He was a fervent Christian, who was known to speak from sunrise to sunset without intermission when exhorting his compatriots to convert to the faith. He, himself, had not always been as temperate as he was devout, but Captain Anderson had cleverly devised a way to cure Assiginack of his addiction to alcohol. One day, when Anderson came upon the chief lying unconscious in a drunken stupor, he bound his hands and feet and then instructed a sickly young boy to sit by his side and look after him. When the powerful chief awoke several hours later, he roared his defiance at whomever had bound him. Believing that his disgrace had been achieved by a weakling while he lay helpless with alcohol, and that he had been ridiculed by all who passed by as he slept it off, he vowed that never again would a drop pass his lips. And none did.

Assiginack's promising son, Francis, did not enjoy the gift of longevity that his father did. A fine linguist and athlete, he took prizes at Upper Canada College in Toronto in the 1840s, then went to work for the Indian Department as clerk and interpreter. When he was stricken with tuberculosis he broke his engagement to a cultured English girl and went home to die. He is buried at Wikwemikong.

Approach

It's about 25 miles, give or take a few depending upon the route you choose, from Killarney to Manitowaning, and closer to thirty if you're coming around from Wikwemikong. Manitowaning Bay, itself, is officially reckoned ten miles long. A strong wind out of the north might be a sailor's delight on this passage, but could be a powerboat's nightmare as the bay funnels to its narrow end. There are no obstructions, but there's no shelter, either, until you reach the village, whither the lighthouse on the hill beckons you from far up the bay.

Dockage and Marine Services

The government dock has been recently rebuilt with floating finger docks in ten feet. Gas, diesel, pumpout and water are supplied, but there is no electricity as yet, and no showers.

Activities for the Crew

Only a block or two from the dock there are a couple of good grocery stores, a liquor and beer store, hardware, bakery, laundromat, restaurant, gift shop, and bank in this village of about 400 people. For dining out Manitowaning Lodge is a pleasant walk of a mile or so from the dock.

The government dock is in the town's waterfront park, with beach, playground, and two unusual historical attractions. The Manitowaning Roller Mill, a gristmill built in 1883, houses displays showing how the land was worked in the old days. Next to the mill the S.S. *Norisle* has found her permanent mooring at a relatively tender age. She was built at Collingwood in 1946 expressly for the ferry run between Tobermory and South Baymouth. With the older *Normac*, which had inaugurated the ferry service in 1932, and later with the *Norgoma*, she carried an annually growing burden of cars and people for the next 27 years. By the early 1970s her hand-fired coal burner was obsolete and her capacity seriously inadequate. When the sleek *Chi-Cheemaun* was launched in 1974 to carry all the ferry traffic, the two older ships were retired. A tour through the *Norisle* will show you how vessels like this operated in the not very distant past. Also in the waterfront complex, the Burns Wharfside Theatre in an old warehouse presents a varied bill of summer performances, in conjunction with the professional Sudbury Theatre Centre.

If you choose the right day to be in Manitowaning you can enjoy harness racing at the track on the edge of town. Near the track are the tennis courts and the Assiginack Historical Museum. The old chief was honored by having the township named for him, and the well arranged museum, housed in an 1857 jail, features Indian artifacts along with those of the white settlers, including a furnished pioneer house, school, and blacksmith shop. The public library occupies the front room of the museum building.

St. Paul's Church is an historic site that still serves its original purpose. A touching plaque inside is inscribed to the memory of Peter Jacob, a missionary who died in 1864 at the age of 31. Jacob was much loved by the Indians, and the memorial is etched in their language as well. Wander among the gravestones in the churchyard, reading the record of the Manitowaning people who were. Take a look at the light-house close up. If you like to walk, there are a number of country roads to follow. About five miles north of town at High Falls there is a pretty one-mile trail along the stream bed to Manitowaning Bay. So closely does the bay come to bisecting the island that a three-mile walk south from town will bring you to the head of South Bay on the open Lake Huron coast. There is a legend of an underground waterway connecting the two bays, which provided quick access to either for Gitchie Manitou, but it has never been found.

Sheguiandah
Chart 2205

Wikwemikong may be the oldest mission in the region and Manitowaning the oldest white settlement on Manitoulin, but the hamlet of Sheguiandah, about fifteen miles north and west from Manitowaning, has these two outranked in antiq-uity by many thousands of years. In the early 1950s archae-ologists unearthed layer upon layer of projectile points and artifacts from a local quartzite bed. Beneath a peat bog evidence was found of quarrying activity that dates back indisputably 9,000 years—long before the North Channel was born. There is another body of scientific opinion that claims an age of 30,000 years for the site. If that is true, it would be one of the oldest habitations of early man in North America.

However long ago prehistoric man inhabited Sheguiandah, modern Indians have been living there for some 150 years, mostly on the adjacent reservation. Their traditions die hard, and the passing of Jim Nahwegizik about twenty years ago was a poignant reminder of the fateful grip upon men's minds of antique beliefs. In 1945 Jim was only 33 years old, home for the summer from his lumbering job on the north shore of Lake Huron. He had always been a healthy, sober, hard working man, but after a few weeks he began to suffer terrible headaches and sleeplessness and quarreled with his mother. He came to the conclusion that she was putting a curse on him—the frightful curse of the Bearwalk. He was certain she had mixed a horrible witches' brew and spat it from her own mouth onto the ground where he would walk, thereby calling forth a devil to take possession of him and cause all kinds of incurable illnesses, including a loss of balance that caused him to lumber like a bear. In a frenzy he ran from his parents' home one night and sought refuge with an aunt and cousin down the road.

His aunt tried to smoke the devils out, but to no avail, and Jim sought the help of a blind, seventeen-year-old witch doctor. He confirmed the diagnosis that Jim was possessed, but his medicine was not strong enough to exorcise the evil spirits. There was only one solution. At three o'clock one morning Jim took his rifle to his parents' home and called for them to come out into the yard. When his father appeared Jim accused him of bearwalking his own son and shot him at close range. His mother ran in terror from the back door of the cabin, but her son did not pursue her. Miraculously, the headache was gone and he went home to sleep soundly for the first time in months.

When he came to trial, a plea of insanity was rejected by the court, and Jim was found guilty of murder. He was sentenced to hang, but his punishment was commuted to life imprisonment. After serving thirteen years as a model prisoner, he came home and hung around the reservation for about three years. Then two years of wandering brought him to Windsor, where he was arrested for breaking parole and returned to prison. He felt better there. There was no life for the likes of him on the outside. But after nine months he was released once more. A year later he was found dead in his bed. His heart, long overburdened with morbid superstition, had given out. You may yet find the abandoned cabin, hidden in a tangled, overgrown yard near the road to Lake Manitou—if you care to look for it. Even the vandals keep clear of this cursed dwelling.

Sheguiandah also has more cheerful sights to see. The Howland-Little Current Historical Museum is there, Canada's first completed centennial project, which artfully presents the life of early settlers in authentic surroundings.

Sheguiandah is not a destination attractive to cruising boats, however. There are several cottage and camping resorts and its marine services are all oriented to small boats.

Approach

From the top of Manitowaning Bay, keep the green spar marking Loon Island Reef to port as you swing around into Sheguiandah Bay. Sheguiandah range lights, at 261°, will direct you to the village, but as you approach O'Meara Point you must shift a bit south to avoid its one-foot shoal. The distance from Manitowaning is about seventeen miles.

Dock

There is a small government dock with seven feet reported alongside, but no facilities. It is rather lost among the resorts and campgrounds with dockage for small boats, launching ramps, and gas. The bay is too exposed for anchorage.

Little Current
Charts 2205 and 2294

Here you are. The bustling Bosporus of the North, where all paths cross, whether by land or by sea. The narrow pass of the North Channel, where the top of Manitoulin almost meets the bottom of the mainland and the highway crosses over on the former railroad bridge. The center from which the roads that link the corners of Manitoulin Island stretch out. The channel through which all ships must navigate that would traverse the North Channel or pass between it and Georgian Bay. The bottleneck with the not so little current that gave the town its start.

George Obbotossaway was a smart young Indian, educated by the missionaries at Manitowaning. Unlike many of his countrymen, he had a shrewd head for business. Early in the 1850s he saw the strategic advantage of locating at the place his people called Wabejong, Place Where the Water

Starts to Run, for the purpose of selling cordwood to the growing number of steamers plying Georgian Bay and the North Channel. They would all have to pass his door; how convenient for them to stop and take on a load of wood. Thither George removed with his Caucasian wife, Sarah Newman, who had been a servant girl in the missionary's home. For several years the family prospered. George opened a store in addition to his cordwood business and built himself a fine frame house.

Alas, the small businessman must ever guard against the depredations of the commercial giants. No less an enterprise than the Company of Adventurers Trading Into Hudson's Bay decided to move its North Channel base from Fort La Cloche on the mainland to the superior location of Little Current. They built a fine post, but not content with merely trading in goods, Mr. McTavish, the trader in charge, began to muscle in on George's steamer fuel supply business. Manitoulin Island was still an Indian reserve and the company had no right to cut cordwood there, George claimed loudly and bitterly to the missionaries. They carried his protest to the government and the Hudson's Bay Company was speedily evicted. So speedily, in fact, that Mr. McTavish never even got to use the store he had built. It served as a charming home for a succession of prominent Little Current families until it burned down in 1942. There's a plaque to mark the site in front of the office of the Ontario Provincial Police, where you can read all about it. Meanwhile, George's business rescue was only temporary. The government decided that the wood belonged to all the Indians in common, so the Indian Department would cut it and peddle it for them.

It wasn't long after this fracas that the Treaty of 1862 opened Manitoulin for white settlement, and Little Current soon had its share of the influx of land-hungry farmers from southern Ontario. The town prospered almost from the start. The logging boom on the North Channel was well under way by the 1880s and Little Current's several sawmills hummed with activity. By 1892 there were complaints that sawdust was polluting the North Channel. Fishermen spread their nets in the productive waters all around and shipped out their catch from the busy wharf to the big cities of North America.

In 1914 a fisherman named La Pointe caught a 275-pound sturgeon, eight feet long, that yielded 57 pounds of caviar. In 1892 Little Current was linked to the outside world by telegraph; in 1896 the Brass Band and Dramatic company was producing smash hits; the curling rink was built in 1904; and movies came in 1909. But most momentous, by far, was the arrival of the railroad in 1914. That was the year they built the final link—the same bridge that swings open to let your boat through on the hour, or that you passed over in your car to reach Manitoulin from Highway 17. In 1945 the roadbed was modified to receive the horseless carriage; the railroad tracks were taken up only in the 1980s.

BOAT'S EYE VIEW OF THE BRIDGE AT LITTLE CURRENT

The last sawmill at Little Current closed in 1924, and by the mid-1950s commercial fishing was finished off. Nor does Little Current supply cordwood any longer to passing steamers. Nevertheless, the same air of activity and "progress" pervades the town, at least in summer. The waterfront is as busy, or perhaps even busier, as in the heyday of the steamships that are all gone now from Georgian Bay and the North Channel. (Occasionally diesel-powered ships unload coal or load iron ore pellets at the CPR wharf on Goat Island.) Their place has been taken by the cruising yachts—hundreds converging every summer on the long waterfront at Little Current or in its marina around the corner.

Their crews spill over into the town, strolling, shopping, visiting, and mingling with hundreds of tourists from resorts and cottages throughout the east end of the island. They began to come, both by land and by sea, in the early 1900s, and their numbers haven't stopped increasing yet. There are those who fear that summer tourists and residents will crowd the farmers off Manitoulin, but that eventuality seems a long way off. Little Current is still an agricultural market town. Its annual cattle sale the last Thursday in September is the largest one-day sale of its kind in Canada.

Don't be misled into expecting a big city when you arrive at Little Current. It may be the center of commercial life on Manitoulin and the largest town, but its permanent population is still less than 1,500 and the main street is barely two blocks long. It's just that compared to the villages and hamlets we've been visiting, Little Current seems bigger and brasher, which it is.

Approach

The local importance of Little Current is eloquently expressed by the fact that it is one of only three towns on all of Lake Huron to have its own, large-scale marine chart—and the other two are four and twelve times larger. Not only does it have a chart, but the approaches to its harbor from both east and west are thoroughly buoyed, belled, and lit with ranges. If you can read a chart and pilot a boat, you can't miss. Only one word of caution is necessary. The current is not little. It can run up to four knots and may be especially treacherous around the pilings of the bridge piers. Furthermore, it reverses itself capriciously through the course of the day. So when passing under the bridge or through the opening, proceed cautiously, with your vessel under control at all times. Closed, the bridge clears at eighteen feet at low water. For taller craft it swings open from a center pivot on the hour and remains open for fifteen minutes. Little Current is about twenty miles from Manitowaning, seven from Sheguiandah by way of the unmarked but relatively clear Strawberry Channel if you follow the charted track.

Dockage and Marine Services

The same current that may plague you at the bridge may also give you embarrassing difficulty at the dock. Or it may be entirely slack, and you'll wonder what I'm talking about. You can judge how fast it's running and in what direction by observing the buoys in the channel to see if they are upright or leaning way over. If the latter, then approach the dock headed into the current, so that you can back down smoothly on a bow line to lay up against the wharf.

All the dockage is end to end along the quarter-mile of government wharf backed up to the main street. Depths are about twenty feet. Although a popular spot, truthfully it isn't always the most comfortable place to lie. There's a fair amount of rolling in the wakes of cruisers coming and going and runabouts running about. You may want to set a small breast anchor to prevent bashing against the dock. Fortunately, the harbor is quiet during sleeping hours, as even here pleasure boats do not run at night. Toward the western end of the dock is a small park that makes the most desirable location for overnight lying. The head and shower building is at the eastern end, as is the launch ramp. Wally's Dock Service sells gas, diesel, and block ice, and operates a couple of pumpout hoses. This area of the dock is for service only, and boats are required to lie elsewhere along the wharf for shopping or overnight docking, once their business with Wally's is concluded. Water and electricity are available along most of the wharf face, except for the two extreme ends. With the heavy demands made on it, however, the electric power may not be delivered to your boat at full strength.

Half a mile west of the government dock, just beyond the flashing white light on Spider Island, is the Little Current Marina. Entered between two rubble breakwalls it has floating slips in six to ten feet. The longest of these slips is thirty feet, and there is little turning radius between their ranks, so larger craft may prefer to lie at the government dock downtown. Electricity and water at dockside, gasoline, water, ice, and pumpout are all supplied here, as are heads and showers in the attractive marina building. The showers have a peculiar disadvantage, however. There is no ventilation in the four individual shower rooms, and the hot water is on a timer. The marina monitors channel 68. There is also a launch ramp here. Urban as is the environment at the government dock, here the atmosphere is country, with picnic tables, tennis courts nearby, a beach, and brilliant sunsets, The one-third mile walk into town is a pleasant one.

Just beyond the west end of the government dock, Boyle's Marina offers haulout on a 12-ton lift or a railway capable of handling 68 feet, full repair services, and boat storage. Its dockage is seasonal. Ferguson Marine, on Highway 6 at the eastern edge of town, services outboards. Harbor Vue Marina, south of Gibbons Point on the eastern approach to Little Current, has seasonal dockage, a launching ramp, gas, and liftout capacity to 38 feet. Golden's Propane Service, a one and a half mile taxi ride, can fill your propane tanks.

Several yacht charterers operate from Little Current, most of whose home offices are located in Sudbury: Discovery Yacht Charters, Finncharters, and Select Yacht Charterers.

Its strategic location, accessibility by highway, several motels, and good supply facilities make Little Current a popular place to pick up and discharge cruising boat guests, change crews, or launch a trailer boat.

Activities for the Crew

Water Street, as Little Current's main street is officially named, presents the full range of commercial services you may need: laundromat (one of the busiest spots in town with cottagers and campers in from miles around), supermarket, drug store, hardware stores, computer and electronics store, gift shops, banks, post office, barber, and bookshop. The modern hospital is two blocks from downtown, and there are several doctors and dentists available. The liquor store and beer warehouse are less conveniently located out on Manitowaning road, Highway 6. Just off that street, still in town, is another good supermarket which, like the one downtown, will deliver to your boat. But the store most famous among cruising people is Turner's.

Back in the 1870s Isaac Turner decided to follow Horace Greeley's advice, but didn't get very far west from the family homestead in southern Ontario before the steamer broke down at Little Current. He and his wife rather liked the little place where they were stuck, so Isaac opened a general store on the hill. As son Byron grew up he entered the family business, followed, in turn by his son, Grant. Grant began the family yachting tradition, and the dockside park honors his memory. The family fortunes progressed through three stores, two of which burned down in typical frontier fashion, before construction of the present building in 1913. Now the second Byron operates the business, plus the summertime store in McGregor Bay, run by Byron number three. The "general" has evolved to "department," and what started as a gift department tucked into a corner has developed into an import shop occupying most of the second floor (the first floor is Stedman's) and featuring Canadian crafts as well. As you mount the stairs, make sure to gaze upward at the handsome array of prints depicting Canada's early history.

Another unique feature of Turner's is the Chart Room, which stocks every nautical publication needed for cruising the North Channel and Georgian Bay, plus a complete set of topographical maps indispensable to the cross-country hiker. Books and publications about the area and the water sports enjoyed here round out the tourist's supply package.

Commercial entertainment in Little Current is pretty well described by eating and drinking, with occasional bingo at the Legion Hall. You can dine pleasantly at the Shaftesbury Steak House on Robinson Street. The 100-year-old building was the home of Thaddeus J. Patten, whose land surveys for the dominion and provincial governments extended throughout the North Channel and Manitoulin. He continued the Bayfield tradition of conferring place names of his own preference, and the one he chose for Little Current was Shaftesbury. That elegant title never captured the fancy of the residents, however, who perpetuated the more descriptive translation from the French translation of the Indian name.

The Anchor Inn, downtown on the site of the old Mansion House, and the Edgewater, next to the laundromat, serve lunches and dinners. Up the hill at the east end of town Dorethy's Place offers tasty home cooking, especially bakery products, in a quaint homey atmosphere, with frilly curtains at the windows. Garr's Family Restaurant is out that way, too. The Shaftesbury and the Anchor Inn have cocktail lounges.

The Anchor Inn also has rooms, and there are four motels: the Wagon Wheel, the Hawberry, the Little Current, and, at the west edge of town, the Sunset.

If you arrive at Little Current the first weekend in August, you will have entertainment aplenty as the Haweaters come home for their annual festival. Why Little Currenters are believed to partake more than others of the bitter fruit of the hawthorne tree is not known for certain, although there is a legend that some early settlers saved themselves from starvation this way. But that doesn't have much to do with the festivities anyway. Over a three-day period they consist of contests, games, dances, concerts, a midway, a fish fry, and, of course, a parade.

West Bay
Chart 2286

After peaking at Little Current, the succession of humps and indentations so characteristic of Manitoulin's north shore continues westward. The next bay is pragmatically designated West Bay. Its major village is known to the Hydrographic Service as Excelsior, in remembrance of the packing material once shipped in large quantities as a by-product of the sawmills, but to the islanders it is West Bay. It is the center of the largest of Manitoulin's six (ceded) Indian reserves and is also the location of the island's single high school. Students attend by bus from Wikwemikong, forty miles to the east, Meldrum Bay, sixty miles west, and all the places in between.

West Bay, like all the others, is wide open to the north and unsuitable for anchorage. It is also free of obstructions. The village at the bottom of the bay, West Bay or Excelsior as you choose, has a small government dock (six feet reported) without any services. What West Bay has to offer the visitor, by either land or sea, is the Ojibwe Cultural Foundation. As part of its program it sponsors fine art and craft work among the people it serves, which is displayed in its gallery and offered for sale. A couple of private shops also sell Indian work along with other Canadian crafts. The Mission Church of the Immaculate Conception is a unique architectural blend of Indian tradition and Christian worship. A twelve-sided structure, the seats are actually steps that descend to a central altar, harking back to the tradition of meeting around a fire pit.

At this point you are twenty miles from Little Current. If you've been driving on Highway 540 you should have taken a break about eight miles ago to hike the Cup and Saucer Trail at the junction with Bidwell Road. You can climb one and one-half miles round trip to the saucer or three miles to the cup. In either case you'll be rewarded with spectacular views of the North Channel, with only two or three really steep stretches. As you stand on top of the escarpment, give a thought to all the little brachiopods and corals who made it for you.

Two miles west of the hiking trail you can let someone else do the walking. Honora Bay Riding Stables, adjacent to Silver Birches Resort, offers guided horse trail rides and overnight cross-country treks.

Kagawong
Charts 2252 and 2257

The next bay west, ten miles from West Bay, thirteen by water, goes by the ungraceful name of Mudge. Lieutenant Bayfield must have thought it a useful name because it could be construed to honor either Lieutenant-Colonel R.E., who was later a boundary commissioner, or Captain Zacharie Mudge, who served with Vancouver on the *Discovery* and later became an admiral. At the foot of the bay with the harsh

British title is a village with a melodic Indian name—
Kagawong, Where Mists Rise from the Falling Waters. Typical
of the whimsies of historical accident, this village is inhabited
largely by whites, while the Indian village in West Bay wears
an English appellation.

Village life began here in 1873, when the Henry brothers,
Robert and William, built a sawmill, store, boarding house,
and later a gristmill. They prospered until they died within
four months of one another in separate ship disasters in 1882.
Robert was one of those who lost his life on the *Manitoulin* in
Manitowaning Bay.

Approach

Mudge Bay is clear and deep. Even McInnes Bank in the
middle, marked by a red and green spar, has a minimum
depth of nine feet. In coming around from West Bay, stay on
the outside of Martin Reef and Gooseberry Island. A white
square tower with a fixed red light marks the harbor.

Dockage and Marine Services

Behind the government wharf there are floating slips with
reported depths in excess of ten feet. Leave the short rubble
breakwater to port on entering. Gas, electricity, water, ice,
pumpout and showers are available. There is also a launching
ramp.

Activities for the Crew

There is a general store, a couple of antique and craft shops,
and a restaurant in the hamlet of just over 100 people, but two
less commonplace attractions provide the reason for visiting
Kagawong. At the head of the harbor is the church of St. John
the Evangelist. Built in 1946, after the congregation spent its
first eight years in an 1898 warehouse, it is known as the
Mariner's Church because of its unusual features. The iron

steering wheel from a lumber boat that sank in the bay some forty years ago hangs over the entrance, and fish net floats adorn the ends of the pews. It is the pulpit that has a special meaning for visiting yachtsmen, for it is the bow section of a sailboat wrecked in a storm off Maple Point in August of 1965. Four of the crew were lost.

As you thoughtfully leave the church, continue around the bay until you come to Kagawong's waterside park, with beach and playground. Then follow the woodland trail leading off to the right along the Kagawong River for about three-quarters of a mile, and you will arrive at one of Manitoulin's most picturesque sights—Bridal Veil Falls. There was a time when

BRIDAL VEIL FALLS, KAGAWONG

the stream was diverted through a concrete flume to generate the island's electric power at the large, unused plant you passed on your way from the dock. When the generating station was discontinued, the bride got her veil back.

For dining out while you're docked at Kagawong, Hideaway Lodge, an attractive American plan resort a few miles out of town at Dutchman Head, will arrange transportation when you call for reservations.

Gore Bay
Charts 2252 and 2257

In the old days, the only connection North Channel folk had with the outside world was by boat. The little ships that made regular calls to all the Channel ports were cherished, and each arrival was enthusiastically greeted by every two- and most of the four-legged residents in town. One of the earliest of these vessels was the steamer *Gore* out of Collingwood. One year, soon after Manitoulin was opened to settlement, she stayed out on her rounds too late. Sheltering from a late fall storm in one of the uninhabited bays of the island's north shore, she soon found herself trapped in the ice for the winter. Curious settlers from the new village of Kagawong came over to look and to anoint the crew to find shelter. For them the place became known as Gore Bay, and when the town site was surveyed for settlement a few years later the name became official. Bayfield's designation, "Janet Cove," was perpetuated in the graceful headland at the entrance to the bay. Who was Janet? He never said.

Gore Bay seemed to attract boat troubles of one sort or another. Only a few decades ago the steamer *Caribou* called to take on a load of Manitoulin cattle. First she docked port side to the government wharf to unload the freight consigned to Gore Bay. Then she moved to the cattle dock to load the waiting beasts on the starboard side. Someone had forgotten to close the portside gangway, however, and several dozen cattle entered the hold, then nonchalantly walked right across the deck and out the other side into the water. They had to be rounded up by rowboat and driven ashore at scattered points, where they proceeded to wander the fields and gardens, with half the town chasing after them. It was an exciting night for all.

Gore Bay, with just under 800 people, is the second largest town on Manitoulin, but its importance far exceeds its size. It is the seat of government—the place of official records, the sitting of the district court twice a month, and the island jail. As befits its status, Gore Bay seems to be a more sober and dignified place than its larger cousin forty miles east. And it has known substantial prosperity from the bounty of field and forest, as the lovely old homes on some of its tree-shaded streets testify. The impressive stone courthouse dates from 1889, when the town was selected for its judicial role, although its interior has been remodeled. The old stone jail, built the same year, was abandoned for that purpose in 1945 in favor of more modern cells. It is now an interesting historical museum.

Somehow Gore Bay has managed to retain more of its historic buildings than many other places. Although that universal scourge, fire, destroyed four of the hotels that served the town before the turn of the twentieth century, one remains. The handsome, thirty-room Queen's Hotel, built in 1880 across from the government dock on what was then Gore Bay's main street, closed its doors to the tourist trade some years ago and is now a private residence. The hotels of Gore Bay were built originally not for the pleasure of vacationists, but to provide temporary housing for new settlers and a home away from home for the commercial travelers who paraded across the island by way of the numerous steamers. Only later did they come to be frequented by summer tourists. Usually they were rollicking places, with individualistic reputations. The Queen's was known especially for its long polished bar, presided over by four bartenders, and the hospitality of its long-time (1912-1940) proprietor, Art "Crusty" Bryan.

For accommodation of contemporary travelers, Gordon's Lodge is open all year and is located on the water at the northeast edge of town, offering both European and American plan. Hill House and The Traveler's Rest offer bed and breakfast.

Gore Bay's airport, the most extensively equipped on the North Channel, makes it a good pickup and discharge point for airborne boat guests. It is also a strategic location for launching a cruising trailer boat because it is the closest Manitoulin jumping-off place for boat camping among the islands. South Benjamin is only fifteen miles away. Gore Bay is also the home of Canadian Yacht Charters, featuring Alohas ranging from 27 to 34 feet.

Approach

Gore Bay, like the others, is wide and deep, once you have passed the intricacies of Clapperton Channel if coming from the east. It's about 18 miles from Kagawong. A fixed red lighted range at 189° is a convenient guide to the village. A pair of red and green spar buoys helps to keep you from shallow water at the point and at the very bottom of the bay.

Dockage and Marine Services

The original government dock, although extended for alongside tieup, is now used mainly for service—gas, diesel, pumpout, ice. Along the waterfront on either side extensive floating dockage accommodation both the local fleet and visiting boats in six-foot depths, with electricity and water at hand. These are not individual slips, but also call for alongside tieup, with each dock accommodating two or more boats. There are two sets of head and shower rooms, one in the old freight shed building and another in a separate building farther down the waterfront. The freight shed is also the site of Canadian Yacht Charters' marine store, where charts are sold along with chandlery of all kinds. The chartering firm operates a travelift for haulout up to 36 feet; mechanical advice is available from service stations in town. A large new building at the waterfront, completed in 1986, houses a Mercury sales and service dealer; additional marine enterprises are expected to take up much of the remaining space.

Activities for the Crew

Gore Bay is a good place to clean up and stock up. it is the last of the urban septet that includes Bruce Mines, Thessalon, Blind River, Killarney, Manitowaning, and Little Current. There is a laundromat, several grocery stores, a natural food store, hardware, drug, gift and clothing shops, liquor store that also sells beer, and a bank, all on Meredith Street, a few blocks from the marina. Barber, hairdresser, doctor, and dentist are all available.

For dining out Gordon's Lodge across the harbor can be reached by dinghy or a pleasant walk around on Water Street. Reservations are requested. The Twin Bluffs Restaurant on Eleanor Street downtown features smorgasbord one night a week. The Galley is a takeout snack bar adjacent to the marina that is open to midnight if you get a late yen.

For entertainment and recreation, you already know about the jail museum, and in an adjacent building is that haven for rainy afternoons, the public library. The waterfront park next to the marina has a visitor information center with restaurant upstairs, tennis courts with night lighting and a ball machine, a children's playground, and a sand beach. A mile or so south of town, the Manitoulin Island Country Club has a nine-hole golf course, rental clubs, snack bar, and cocktail lounge. Just plain walking around town is a pleasant pastime; there are some colorful gardens to admire. For more serious hiking there are two three-mile walks along either shore of the bay. The road to Janet Head on the marina side follows the waterfront to the pretty lighthouse, now a private home. The east bluff road follows the ridge for spectacular views from the two cleared lookouts. Movies are shown on weekends in the community hall, and several festivals take place during the summer that include games, craft displays, entertainment, dancing, and food.

In addition, Gore Bay offers one service that is unique on the island—car rental at Bordie's Fleet and Leasing. You might welcome a change of pace from the cruising boat, but, more important, here is your chance to roam the intriguing interior of Manitoulin Island. The scene varies from rolling farm and meadow to mixed pulpwood bush, from Great Lake vista to forest-girt inland lake intimacy. Huge gray barns with log outbuildings guard the farmsteads behind silvery split rail fences with stiles to allow humans to move from field to field, but not animals. On Manitoulin the general store still lives, and there are picnic tables at intervals for you to enjoy the lunch you bought in one of them. There is not a single traffic light on the island, yet the roads are well signed, with indicators for each tourist sight and resort. Along much of the

MANITOULIN ROADSIDE

roadside Manitoulin's limestone is stacked in slabs that look like quarried stones waiting for pickup by a passing truck. And everywhere along the unsprayed shoulders the wildflowers sing their welcome.

The Interior
Turner's Manitoulin Map

Gore Bay is at the approximate center of the island on an east-west axis—a good place from which to make a circuit by car. If you travel west, however, there is no circuit to be made. This is the narrowest and least developed part of the island. You'll go and come back on the same road, Route 540. There are a few dirt side roads to get you among the farms, the little villages like Evansville and Burpee, and through the bush to some of the remote bays on the Lake Huron shore—Murphy Harbour, Misery Bay, and Burnt Island Harbour. This is not the tourist part of Manitoulin Island, for most of the land is wild, with farms clustered near some of the villages. Much of the land is owned by Ontario Paper Company, to feed pulpwood to its plants elsewhere. Every so often you'll pass a little building marked "Hunt Club." That's the other thing the bush is good for. On the side road to Burnt Island Harbour there is a mink farm.

Overnight accommodations and restaurants are nonexistent west of Campbell Bay, until you get to the modest Meldrum Bay Hotel at the end of the line, 45 miles west of Gore Bay. Although there are no "attractions" as such, a drive through this end of the island will give you a feel for the old Manitoulin, relatively undisturbed by the intrusions of mid-twentieth century tourists and clangor.

The attractions on Route 540 east of Gore Bay to Little Current have already been described in the section for West Bay. On this road you are traveling along the high shores of the North Channel much of the time, and there are some impressive vistas to be enjoyed. If the day is clear take a side trip out to Maple Point or Dutchman Head.

Maple Point was the scene of a bizarre tragedy fifty years ago. Young Daniel Dodge, son of John Dodge of automotive fame, was quite a different character from the rest of his rather notorious family. He liked to tinker with motors and he loved the north country, especially the lodge he owned at Maple Point on Manitoulin Island. While living there he met and fell in love with Laurine MacDonald, the telephone operator at Gore Bay and daughter of a tugboat captain. On August 3, 1938, a few days after Danny's twenty-first birthday, he and nineteen-year-old Laurine were married. The small wedding took place at Meadowbrook Hall, near Rochester, Michigan, the baronial estate of his mother, Mrs. Alfred Wilson. The bridal couple left immediately for their honeymoon, a tour of northern Ontario by car and trailer, ending up at Maple Point Lodge.

One afternoon Danny was working in the garage with Laurine's cousin Lloyd Bryant, an employee of the estate. Wondering whether some old sticks of dynamite that had been lying around for years were still good, Danny lit one of them and threw it out the window. But he missed his mark. The stick hit the window frame and rebounded back into the garage before it exploded. Danny and Lloyd were critically injured in the blast; Laurine and another employee, Frank

Valiquette, were less severely burned. Because the road to Kagawong was so bad, Laurine decided that the fastest way to reach the hospital at Little Current was in Danny's 28-foot speedboat. She took the wheel for the 18-mile trip. About half way along in choppy seas, Danny, delirious with pain, suddenly stood up in the boat, lost his balance and fell overboard. The anguished bride, injured herself, circled and circled to no avail.

A couple of weeks later the body was recovered by two Little Current fisherman, who received the $1,500 reward offered by the Dodge family for its recovery. The sequel to the tragedy was legal wrangling over Laurine's right to Danny's $10 million inheritance. She eventually was awarded most of it, and later remarried and settled in the United States. Whether Laurine spent much, if any, time at the blighted lodge we don't know, but she didn't sell it until 1961.

On a more cheerful note, at Dutchman Head is Hideaway Lodge, an American plan resort with a sand beach and boats and motors for rent.

If you're making the circuit of the eastern part of the island, you have several routes to choose from. Route 6 from Little Current to South Baymouth has also been described, but you don't want to stick to the main highways. From Route 6, about two miles west of Manitowaning, take the Bidwell Road around the north shore of Lake Manitou, the island's largest inland lake. Its beauties and its fish were discovered early in this century by such millionaires from the United states as the brother of Vice President Dawes and oil magnate J.C. Trees. These men built luxurious "cottages" on the lake for their wives and families, with additional cottages for servants and guests. Mr. Trees was known to charter a steamship to bring him and his entourage to Manitoulin, complete with brass band. That kind of opulent display being no longer in fashion, the contemporary cottages on Lake Manitou are of a much more modest sort, as are the housekeeping and camping resorts. Red Lodge is the one American plan resort on this side of the lake. The Bidwell Road connects with Highway 540 near the Cup and Saucer Trail, and you can return to Gore Bay by it or turn south on Route 551 for another circular drive, to be described a little later on.

Another turnoff from Route 6 occurs at 542 near Tehkummah, about eight miles north of South Baymouth and about eleven miles from Manitowaning. A mile or so from route 6 you are faced with two choices. The left fork will carry you through the farm village of Tehkummah, named for Indian Chief Louis Tekoma, Rays of Light Flashing in the Sky. Continuing west, you will be driving alternately through farm and bush country. About a mile past the Manitou River bridge (a very small one), a sign and small parking lot direct you to the one and one-half mile Carnarvon-Tehkummah trail (sometimes rather soggy) to the Lake Huron shore at Michael Bay. Once a thriving resort, the Bay View Hotel here attracted large numbers of Americans in the 1880s. Now all is quiet and almost wild again, with only a few anglers disturbing the gulls and watching Lake Huron roll in.

Twelve miles altogether from Tehkummah on the main road brings you to Providence Bay. The Pacific Hotel here rivaled the Bay View in the eighties, but it, too, is gone. Unlike Michael, Providence Bay remains a resort village. The Indian name for the place is Be-be-ko-da-wan-gog, Where the Singing Sand Curves Around the Water. Indeed it does. Here is the largest and smoothest beach on Manitoulin, a great curving arc one doesn't expect to find in this part of the world. The water is shallow for a considerable distance out into the bay, making it a safe place for children to swim. And a popular family vacation spot it is, with a tenting and trailer camp, a number of housekeeping cottages, and a beachside park. In the village, the Huron Sands Motel offers modern rooms and a good dining room. Connected with the motel is one of the most generously stocked Canadian craft shops in the north country. Providence Bay hosts a big agricultural fair in August.

The road north from Providence Bay joins up with Route 542 about three miles from town. You can turn west for the return trip to Gore Bay, following 542 all the way for about twenty miles from Providence Bay. This is, frankly, one of the least scenic stretches of Manitoulin's road network, so you might want to turn off on the Perivale road north out of Spring Bay to the south shore of Kagawong Lake and follow that west to connect with 542 again at Long Bay. Kagawong Lake has several campgrounds and a large number of resorts around its shores. Most offer housekeeping cabins; Long Bay Lodge has American plan accommodations.

Remember the fork just before Tehkummah, where you took the left road? If you turn to the right, instead, you pass one of Manitoulin's unique enterprises, Dove Industries. Here exquisitely crafted sailing and rowing boats are fashioned from epoxy stabilized Manitoulin white cedar. Stop in for a tour of the shop and to learn what new ideas Ian Ross is generating.

Continuing on, you soon reach the village of Sandfield, where Lake Manitou drains into the Manitou River. There is a fish hatchery here that produces most of the stock for Manitoulin's lakes and rivers—rainbow and speckled trout and smallmouth bass. Visitors are welcome. Route 542 comes close to the shore of Lake Manitou only where it passes between that large body of water and much smaller Big Lake to the south of it. There is a dirt road that branches off to the north about a mile before that, at Long Lake, which also leads to Lake Manitou and the rustic American plan Timberlane Lodge. At the narrows between Manitou Lake and Big Lake you can turn right at the Rockville Road and follow it northward around the west shore of Lake Manitou. After about twelve miles it connects with the Bidwell Road near the Cup and Saucer Trail, and you're back on the main line 540.

If you don't turn onto the Rockville Road, you will find yourself after a few miles at the town of Mindemoya. This is the most important place in the interior, the market center for the large farming region all around it. If you've been buying butter and cream on the island, here is where it came from. The town is a social center, too, with dances at the community hall and bingo at the arena. There are two restaurants. The Island Hub serves full lunches and dinners, and Grandma Lee's Bakery serves sandwiches in addition to its pastries. The most remarkable thing in Mindemoya and the place people travel a distance to see is the church.

St. Francis of Assisi looks as though it was plucked from a twelfth century setting in an English country town and set down bodily in this remote corner of Canada. But look again. That authentic Norman design was constructed of Manitoulin limestone a mere fifty years ago. Led by their Pastor, Reverend Richard Taylor, the local parishioners built the handsome edifice with their own hands during a severe depression. Word of their painstaking efforts reached the ears of their Anglican brethren on the other side of the Atlantic. Help and encouragement flowed back across the sea in a most unusual form. Ancient treasures from the cathedrals and palaces of England were donated to furnish the little house of worship so far away. The altar hangings were hand embroidered by the ladies in waiting to Queen Elizabeth I and had graced Kensington Palace chapel for over 300 years. St. Francis' worshippers are called to service by a bronze bell donated by the Lord's Commissioners of the Admiralty. And the statue above the altar was the personal gift of His Majesty, King George V, from the Palace of Westminster. Visit the church to see all of its exquisite and venerable objects and to admire the workmanship of the structure itself.

On leaving Mindemoya you can take Route 551 north along the eastern shore of the lake of the same name, to link up with Route 540 at West Bay about seven miles away. Only a mile out of Mindemoya along this route, the Ketchankookem Trail goes off to the left, to follow the south shore of Lake Mindemoya for a while and then reconnect with 542. On this road is the Brookwood Brae Golf Course, nine holes, with rental clubs, a snack bar and cocktail lounge.

Route 551 is the most thickly developed stretch of lakefront on the island, with a series of cottage resorts. For a more scenic return to Route 540 and Gore Bay, follow the Ketchankookem Trail around until it meets 542, or simply take 542 out of Mindemoya in the first place. It borders the southern tip of Lake Mindemoya for a stretch. Shortly after 542 leaves the lakeshore there will be a road off to the right. This is the one to follow up the beautiful, wooded west shore of the lake. As you travel you will have a splendid view of Treasure Isle, the high island that gave the lake its name. Legend tells that long ago an old Indian chief became enraged when his wife ruined the pot of potent stuff he was brewing for a council meeting. He was so angry that he kicked her off the cliff near their campsite and she landed in the lake, where she became an island shaped like an old woman on her hands and knees. Ever after the lake was known by her presence—Mindemoya, Old Woman.

There is an American plan resort on this road, Rock Garden Terrace, with excellent food and a swimming pool as well as lake swimming. The name is not whimsical. The property was originally owned by John Miller of Odessa, Missouri, who summered here for thirty years between 1911 and 1941. His hobby was gardening. From the top of the bluff he carved terraced flower beds out of the limestone, filled them with soil, and then constructed a winding trail of stone steps among the beds leading down to the bluff's edge overlooking the lake. The immense variety of flowers and herbs he planted was watered by pipes built into the beds through which water was pumped up from the lake. And for lovers there was a special seat built of large, flat stones where they could sit and enjoy the view together. As his masterpiece of art and engineering progressed he opened it to the public. But after the property was sold and resold a few times the gardens were closed and the plantings fell into decline. Rock Garden Terrace resort maintains the paths, however, and there are still hardy perennial plantings to admire, so be sure to walk the garden of stone when you stop.

Half a mile beyond the lodge is another marked Carnarvon Township hiking trail, leading through woods and an open plain. The nine-mile stretch up the west side of Lake Minde-moya to Route 540 at Billings completes the last of the circular routes around the interior of Manitoulin. You may not be able to do them all, but be sure to sample at least one that takes you through the rolling farm country enclosed by Routes 6 and 542, within the embrace of Providence Bay, Mindemoya, and Tehkummah. Here is where you get a real sense of the agricultural life of the island that dates back over a hundred years to the first settlers. Many of their log cabins are still standing in this part of the island, a few still occupied. And the miles of silver split-rail fences are, in many cases, originals that go back for generations. Dairying is important here and the cows seem to gaze at you with friendlier faces than they do elsewhere in the world. It is a special part of Manitoulin that shouldn't be missed if you're out by car.

Although the longest circuit eastward from Gore Bay is only a little over a hundred miles, excluding any side trips, don't be deceived by the relatively short distances between places. The roads on Manitoulin are two-lane asphalt with plenty of curves, and some of the offbeat roads you want to explore are gravel (i.e., sharp limestone) or dirt. So for safety, comfort, and enjoyment of what you came to see, don't expect to average more than thirty miles an hour. If you're renting a car out of Gore Bay, you might consider stopping overnight at one of the resorts in the interior, in order to make your trip more leisurely. If you're traveling by car in the first place, your pace and itinerary will be determined by where you elect to take lodgings or camp, and for how long. In either case, a picnic lunch may be advisable. Especially in the southern and western farm-bush parts of the island, there are no little roadside restaurants to drop into for a midday meal. If your itinerary doesn't take you through a town at lunchtime or to a resort with dining room for dinner, you'd better pack your own.

Bayfield Sound
Charts 2252 and 2258

Around Janet Head to the west is a large, protected body of water, roughly twelve miles by five, whose shores reproduce the North Channel in miniature. Bayfield Sound is enclosed by Barrie Island and indents the Manitoulin coast with a series of bays. But Barrie Island is not really an island. It is a large, low-lying peninsula connected to the rest of Manitoulin by a narrow neck of land, hardly wider than the road which crosses it. The isthmus is enough, however, to require the westbound cruising boat to make a wide sweep of about eighteen miles in order to enter the sound from the west end of Barrie. Thus Julia Bay, next over from Gore and named for the daughter of a friend of Lieutenant Bayfield, is a snare and a deception. It doesn't lead to Bayfield Sound and the only possible anchorage, in its southwest corner, is unpleasantly close to the airport. Smith Bay, in the southeast corner of Julia, is wide open to the northwest. Nor does the north shore of Barrie Island offer anything to detain the cruising boat.

The Bayfield family guards the entrance to their sound. Papa's island is, of course, Henry; Fanny is mama; and daughter, Gertrude Island, lies beyond and between them. Most of the scenery and facilities are to be found at the eastern end of the sound, on the south side. The lieutenant's mother, Elizabeth, had a lovely bay named for her, but his sister, Helen, was awarded the prize in this area. The Barrie Island shore is shoal and Rozels Bay is too close to the airport for comfortable anchorage.

Because of the distances to the desirable destinations at the eastern end of Bayfield Sound—thirty miles from Gore Bay, forty from Meldrum Bay—and the flukey winds one often encounters here, the sound is more appealing to power-boaters than to sailors.

Approach

Heron Patch and Jubilee Shoal are two unmarked reefs on the approach to Bayfield Sound. If coming from the east keep half to three-quarters of a mile off the Barrie Island shore and you will easily avoid them. As you round the island keep well off until past Horace Point Bank off Fishery Point. Then you will see the red spar off the group of family islands that guides you into the clear water of the sound. If you're coming from the west you can head directly for the spar, after rounding Cape Roberts.

Dockage and Marine Services

Northernaire is an attractive American plan resort at the foot of Campbell Bay, with a warm welcome for cruising boats. Finger docks, with seven-foot depths, are protected by a breakwall. Gas, water, electricity, ice, heads, and showers are available. In addition, visiting boat crews are extended the privileges of the family resort—sand beach, playground, shuffleboard court, and, of course, the dining room. Should you want to base here for trailer boating, there is a launching ramp. You might also want to take a dinghy under the bridge into Wolsey Lake, where the fishing is excellent.

The only other dockage in Bayfield Sound is at the western end in Cook's Bay, at the small government dock. Watch for deadheads as you approach it, and moor only at the outer end in six feet. There are no services here.

Anchorage

There are only two well-protected anchorages in Bayfield Sound. One, under Scott's Bluff between Helen and Campbell Bays, has been for many years the province of Camp Adanac (try it backwards), a fine boys' camp. Its small boat docks and swimming area occupy most of the cove. On the other side of Helen Bay there is scenic shelter under Ned Island in ten feet over mud. The only hazards in approaching this island are the reefs off the northern tip. If you stay 150 yards or so offshore, you'll have no trouble. There is a house on the mainland. Courtesy, and the contour of the bottom, suggest that you anchor closer to the island.

Vidal Bay
Charts 2252 and 2258

Vidal is not typical of the succession of bays that march across Manitoulin. It is shallow, in contour not depth, and enclosed by an island at its mouth. It is also quite uninhabited; perhaps it doesn't look very different than it was when viewed by Lieutenant Bayfield's assistant, for whom it was named. At any rate, it is still a pretty place, about eighteen miles from Bayfield Sound, but not very well protected for anchorage. The best place to drop your hook is in the mud of the southwest corner. In low water years there's a little sand beach.

Meldrum Bay
Charts 2251 and 2252

Keeping a lighthouse in the old days was steady work that required a man to be conscientious in the performance of his duties. But it didn't occupy all his time. So William Cullis, second keeper of the Mississagi Light that guided ships through the perilous strait of the same name along the western coast of Manitoulin Island, took to building sailboats for the Indians. Strolling up the shore one day back in the 1890s, on the lookout for good mast trees, he spied something even better—a snowshoe rabbit darting into a hole under the upturned roots of a blown down tree. With visions of the rabbit steaming on a platter, Cullis plunged after him, but his eye was arrested yet again. Something glinted there in the tangled roots of the tree and, to his astonishment, it turned out to be part of a watch chain. Sure enough, after digging a few minutes in the gravel below, he found the large brass watch. Along with it were some old coins.

Now finding treasures such as this, which obviously might have washed ashore from some wreck, was not especially unusual. It was precisely because there were so many wrecks in these waters that the government had built the lighthouse in 1873. But to find these things under the roots of a large tree! That was something else again. So may Cullis have thought as he rubbed the dirt off the old coins. Then his eyes did pop in amazement. The coins bore a *fleur de lis*, and the date on them was sixteen-seventy-something. The rabbit was forgotten as Cullis continued to search the area. Then he noticed a small cave. Perhaps he was becoming inured to surprises, but surely he was at least startled when he entered and beheld the grisly sight—four skeletons lying in a row.

Was this the remains of the crew from the old wreck that had been lying half-submerged off the beach a couple of miles north of the lighthouse ever since the earliest settlers could remember? They had been making harrow points from the derelict's iron spikes and bolts for years, and the Indians had shown them how to burn the timbers to get lead from the caulking for making fish line sinkers. It had been a useful wreck until it slid off the beach in a fearful storm one night. Now Lightkeeper Cullis had apparently found the crew where they had taken shelter, only to freeze or starve.

When he came back in a boat with his assistant, John Holesworth, they found more coins, a couple of brass cannon rams, and a few shipwright's tools. They took their treasures and the four skulls back to the lighthouse, and for years the curious came to look at the display. The coins and other small objects were kept in a baking powder can, while the skulls were set up in a row for decoration along the lighthouse dock.

The excitement of the find soon wore off for the few local farmers. But when Frederick W. Major, successively school teacher, newspaper publisher, and police magistrate at Gore Bay, came to see it years later, interest revived again. Major was an educated man who knew his country's history. He immediately speculated that the wreck and its refugee skeletons might solve one of the most tantalizing mysteries on the Great Lakes—the disappearance of the *Griffon*, first ship to sail the upper lakes. She was built at Niagara in 1679 by René Robert Cavelier, Sieur de la Salle. As unlucky as her owner, the forty-foot barque was lost on her maiden voyage. She had reached her original destination at Green Bay, where La Salle and his associates disembarked to explore overland, while the *Griffon* took on a load of furs to carry back to Niagara to satisfy his voracious creditors. She never arrived. Ever since the day in September of 1679, when she was last sighted by some Indians on the north shore of Lake Michigan tearing eastward before a gale, the world has wondered what became of her. Had it now found out?

Major knew that there were six men aboard the ill-fated ship, but Cullis had found only four skeletons. Sure enough, a further search revealed two more in another cave. The most convincing evidence, in addition to the buttons and coins, was the size of one of the skulls. It was enormous. One local wag liked to cover half of his face with just the jaw bone. The *Griffon* had been commanded by a blasphemous scoundrel, Captain Luke Dare, known as Luke the Dane. The man was seven feet tall.

Still, all of this wasn't proof that the *Griffon* had been found. Other knowledgeable men followed Major to the remote lighthouse to view the relics, and later to send divers down to examine the wreck itself. Samples of the iron work and timbers were sent off to be authenticated by experts. The most conclusive statement that has been pried out of any of them over the years is that the iron *could* have been fashioned in the seventeenth century and the timbers *could* have come from oaks indigenous to the Niagara peninsula. To add to the puzzle, the Mississagi wreck has a rival. The late Orrie Vail of Tobermory, eighty miles southeast, was certain that the relics he recovered from Russell Island and displayed in his shop were the genuine remains of the *Griffon*, and he convinced a number of historians. His evidence may have been as good as that at Mississagi. Not until a carved griffon from the bow or stern, or one of the ship's anchors or cannon is raised, will the controversy and the mystery be laid to rest.

Meanwhile, the bones and skulls of the unfortunate crew have been lost, the dockside decorations long since kicked into the water. And the watch, along with many of the coins and buttons, disappeared years ago from the baking powder can—even the can is gone. In 1942 the main body of the wreck was cast by a storm from the near shore shoals into the deepest water of the strait, 35 fathoms down. As the evidence disappears, hope for finding proof is dim, though not abandoned.

Some of the artifacts recovered by research divers are on display in the museum at Gore Bay. At one time there were many more in the Griffon Museum that Tom Tomlinson set up near his home in Meldrum Bay. He was as firm in his belief in the authenticity of his *Griffon* as Orrie Vail was in his. But old Tom is gone now, too, and his widow, unable to carry on his campaign, closed the museum, along with the little game farm they used to operate across the road, and gave the precious objects to the Gore Bay Museum. And there the tale hangs—unresolved unless and until a heavily financed expedition sends divers down successfully to the stormy deeps of Mississagi Strait to find a grotesque mythical beast, half eagle, half lion, who may yet be crouching there.

If the crew of the first ship to sail these waters missed safety in the haven of Meldrum Bay by less than a dozen miles, present-day sailors do not. This last indentation of the Grand Manitoulin, just around the hump of the island from Mississagi Strait, is a popular port of call. For American cruising boats entering the North Channel, it is where they check in with the Canadian government. For those on their way home, it is the last village.

Like Killarney at the other end of the Channel, the remoteness of Meldrum Bay has helped to preserve its quaint identity. It is a tiny hamlet—barely sixty people live here— spread out on the hillside above the bay. Farming the thin, stony soil brought heartbreaking disappointment to many of the settlers at this end of the island. Such prosperity as they enjoyed came mainly from logging and fishing. Rarely does a fishing tug put out from Meldrum Bay any more, however, and there is no longer a sawmill.

Approach

The only obstruction in Meldrum Bay, about 35 miles direct from Gore Bay, is Batture Island and its shoal. These are marked, respectively, by a flashing white light and a red spar, and should give no trouble. If you're coming from Vidal Bay there is a channel marked with a pair of red and green spars at Chamberlain Point, but the approach to it from offshore is foul. Three miles from the spar off Batture Island you'll arrive at the village, where a fixed red light will guide you in if you're caught after dark.

HEADING FOR THE DOCK, MELDRUM BAY

Dockage and Marine Services

The good old government dock, complete with white freight building, is here to greet you. The floating docks, with alongside tieup in six feet or more, on the south side of the L-shaped dock accommodate the large number of boats that put in here in season. Gasoline, diesel, electricity, water, ice, pumpout, and charts are all available dockside. There is no suitable protected anchorage in the bay, but there is a launching ramp for trailer boats. Because of its distance from the North Channel's main cruising grounds Meldrum is not recommended as a place to launch, however. Boat crews are welcome to use the heads, showers, and laundromat at the campground, a short walk from the dock.

Actvities for the Crew

There are two general stores in town. Meldrum Bay Outfitters near the dock sells liquor; Meeker's on the hill houses the post office in a building that dates from 1900. Mike Meeker, who also operates the marina, offers a rare form of entertainment to visitors—trips to the town dump about 9:00 each evening to see Yogi Bear come out of the woods to forage. Across the road from the store the Harbour Cafe at the campground offers lunches and snacks on home-baked bread. Next door to Meeker's is Meldrum Bay's most imposing building, the Meldrum Bay Inn, built in 1906. Owners Steve and Sam offer unique hospitality. He turns out delicious Hungarian cooking, and she sells her unusual paintings. They also provide takeout home-baked bread, deli that includes home-made sausage, and portable menu items.

If you're traveling by car, the Inn is where you'll put up for the night, and you can drive out to Mississagi Lighthouse to recall its memories. It was automated in 1970 and is now a museum, with a snack bar, a campground, and hiking trails. The hardy folk who come by boat can hike the seven miles just to get there, or inquiry of the dockmaster may get you motorized transport. If you don't care to wander so far, there are more leisurely walks to be enjoyed on the country roads around Meldrum Bay. The Net Shed Museum, featuring the furnishings and memorabilia of the early settlers, completes the round of entertainments.

Cockburn Island
Charts 2251 and 2267

At Meldrum Bay you have reached the end of Manitoulin Island, but, happily, not quite the last of the North Channel. Less than twelve miles to the west lies the harbor for the old Petit Manitoulin. It was probably Bayfield who changed the name to honor Vice-Admiral Sir George Cockburn, later Lord of the Admiralty. Or it could have been named for Lieutenant-Colonel Francis Cockburn, Deputy Quartermaster General, who attended the Earl of Dalhousie on an inspection tour of the area in 1822. Either was a worthy man for this worthy island, a felicitous finale to a North Channel cruise.

Actually, Cockburn Island was settled before the west end of Manitoulin. The first person of record on the island was an American, Siberon Tolsma, known as Sebe, from Cheboygan, Michigan. From about 1878 to 1885 he operated a thriving fishery, shipping the catch in his two boats, *Messenger* and *Dispatch*, out of the bay and village that bear his name. By the time he left, logging was well under way. Virtually all the timber rights on the island were held by a succession of American companies. Ontario Paper Company acquired most of them in 1947, and was the first to manage the island for sustained yield. At the present time it has leased cutting rights to hardwood and pulpwood to the Midway Lumber Company of Thessalon, to supply their mills there. As the forest was cleared in the eighties and nineties, farm families came in to settle the fertile land. The population peaked at 1,000 before World War I, and there were two schools to serve the children.

But all that is past. The last school closed in 1961, the farm children moved on to less isolated places as they grew up, logging crews came in only temporarily to work the forest, and the last couple in residence left in 1969. By then and for several years thereafter, Tolsmaville was a ghost town of the

Old West variety—where the furniture stood in many of the houses just as it was left, with even a jam pot or a salt shaker still on the kitchen table. Then, in the mid-1970s there began a returning to Cockburn Island, at first for fall hunting and spring fishing, later for summer recreation. Most of the people who come regularly are descended from island families retaining title to their houses. In August of 1981 they assembled on the island for a gala two-day centennial celebration. It is still an organized township with elected officers, and once again a hardy couple or two live there the year round. Even in summer, the electric generator operates mainly during the evening.

The logging trails and the old farm roads provide miles of easy hiking. All over the island farm buildings stand in a state of suspended animation, old lilacs and hollyhocks bloom, and the fields are not yet fully overgrown. Wildlife abounds in the fields and in the acres upon acres of forest. McQuaig's Hill, the highest point of the island, has a fire lookout tower with a splendid view. In a word, Cockburn is a place to roam, a last fling at uncluttered, uninhabited nature. But it requires special awareness of her greatest enemy, fire, and special courtesy from the visitor who may enjoy peeking in windows. Remember to respect the privacy and closed doors of the houses; they do belong to someone.

Approach and Dock

For a near ghost town, Tolsmaville is very well marked. Of course the lumber boats must come in and out all the time. The approach is deep and clear, and beacons in line at 169° lead you to the breakwater with a red and white daymark, topped by a flashing red light. You will pass another wharf west of it, extending northward into the bay with a flashing white light at its tip. That is where the company boats dock, but it is too exposed for pleasure craft. Go around the end of the breakwater-wharf to find a place at one of the floating docks perpendicular to it in eight-foot depths, or else fender your boat well and tie alongside the concrete government dock. Here you're protected from all winds. Anchorage behind the breakwater is also possible, but holding may be poor in some places where the bottom is fouled with sawdust and logs. There are, needless to say, no services.

And now, have we come regretfully to the end of the story? Not quite. There is yet a postscript. The last little bonus isn't *exactly* in the North Channel, but for those who are reluctant to leave, or late on entering, it is close enough and like enough to belong to the Channel in spirit.

Around the corner from Tolsmaville, fourteen miles away in False DeTour Passage, Cockburn Island sprouts a satellite—Kitchener Island. Behind it is a delightful, remote, usually uninhabited anchorage. Just follow the shore of Cockburn, keeping about half a mile off to avoid little Herschell Island and its reefs. Anchorage between Kitchener and Cockburn is open to the north, so if your draft allows you to cross a bar with a low water depth of four feet, continue on down between the two islands until you are abeam of a gravel beach with a clump of cedars behind it. Then turn west and drop your hook in the fully protected cove in the east shore of Kitchener. Be sure to make the turn at the cedar clump, as there is a rock close to the surface just beyond.

Dinghy across to the gravel beach for a campfire or walk in the woods, but if the owners of the one cottage here should be in residence, observe the usual courtesies. If you're boat camping and have had enough of towns, here is the last bit of North Channel rock to pull up on and pitch your tent.

And that's it. The very last.

Appendices

Appendix A
Tables of Distance
(in miles)

By Land

	Place to Place	Cumulative
Bruce Mines		
Thessalon	11	
Blind River	33	44
Spragge	17	61
Spanish	11	72
Massey	13	85
Espanola	20	105
Killarney	112	217
Birch Island	15	120
Little Current	13	133
Sheguiandah	7	140
Manitowaning	14	154
Wikwemikong	10	164
South Baymouth	18	182
Cup and Saucer Trail	20	202
via Bidwell Road		
Tehkummah	11	165
Providence Bay	13	178
Gore Bay	26	204
Sandfield	4	169
Mindemoya	12	181
Billings via west	15	196
shore Mindemoya		
Lake		
West Bay	7	188
Little Curront	20	208
Kagawong	9	197
Gore Bay	10	207
Campbell Bay	12	219
Meldrum Bay	34	253

By Water

	Place to Place	Cumulative
Milford Haven		
Hilton Beach	15	
Portlock Harbour	3	18
Picture Island	6	21
Richards Landing	5	26
Killaly Cove	5	31
Portlock Harbour	5	36
Bruce Mines	8	44
MacBeth Bay	14	58
Thessalon	16	60
East Grant Island	16	76
Mississagi Bay	8	84
Blind River	9	93
Clara Island, east end	9	102
Turnbull Harbour	2	104
Long Point Cove	4	108
Serpent Harbour	7	115
John Harbour	7	111
Beardrop Harbour	3	114
Lett Island Anchorage	4	118
Moiles Harbour	7	121
Coursol Bay	5	126
Aird Island Anchorage	8	134
Thomas Island	8	129
Spanish	4	133
Shoepack Bay	5	138
Armour Island	4	142
Eagle Harbour	2	144
Oak Bay, entrance	5	143
McBean Harbour	5	148
McTavish Island	5	153
Notch Bay	6	159
Fox Harbour	4	152
Benjamin and Croker	6	158
Logan Bay	4	162
Clapperton Harbour	8	170
Amedroz Island	6	164
Bedford Island Harbour	6	170
Bell Cove	5	175
LaCloche Channel, south end	7	182

By Water

	Place to Place	Cumulative
Birch Island Landing	4	186
Whitefish Falls	5	191
Flat Point	8	199
Little Current	10	180
McGregor Point	13	193
The Anchorage	8	201
Frazer Point	3	196
Mary Ann Cove	2	198
The Pool	9	207
Boyle Cove	4	200
Blueberry Island	6	206
Browning Cove	10	216
Snug Harbour	7	223
Portage Couvert	7	230
Killarney	2	232
Wikwemikong	16	248
Manitowaning	28	276
Sheguiandah	16	292
Little Current	8	300
West Bay, village	20	320
Kagawong	14	334
Gore Bay, village	17	351
Ned Island	26	377
Campbell Bay	6	383
Vidal Bay	30	381
Meldrum Bay	8	389
Tolsmaville	13	402
Kitchener Island	14	416

Appendix B

Resort, Motel, and Marine Accommodations

(west to east on the north shore; alphabetical on Manitoulin Island)

North Shore

Place by Post Office Address   Services

Richard's Landing POR 1JO
Government Dock, Paul's Marina   Gas, electricity, water,
                                                            pumpout, launch ramp

Hilton Beach POR 1GO
Government Dock, Hilton Beach   Gas, electricity, water,
Marine and Sports   pumpout, launch ramp

Bruce Mines POR 1CO
K's Restaurant and Motel, Box 74   Dining room
Garnet Motel, Box 133
Bruce Mines Marina   Gas, diesel, pumpout, ice,
                                                           water, electricity, heads,
                                                           showers, launch ramp

Thessalon POR 1LO
Belle Isle Motel, Box 209
Carolyn Beach Motel, Box 10   Dining room, beach
Golden Rooster Motel, Box 53   Dining room, beach
Government Dock, Bill's Marine   Gas, diesel, water, ice,
                                                           electricity, pumpout,
                                                           heads, showers, propane,
                                                           charts, launch ramp

Blind River POR 1BO
Edgewater Inn, Box 1898   Dining room
North Shore Inn, Box 219   Dining room, indoor pool,
                                                          sauna
Old Mill Motel, Box 251   Beach
Vajda Motel, Box 598   Dining Room

Place by Post Office Address	Services
Blind River Marina	Gas, diesel, pumpout, electricity, water, ice, heads, showers, charts, car & bicycle rental, launch ramp
Spragge POR 1KO	
Marcel Motel, Box 36	
North Channel Yacht Club	Gas, water, electricity, pumpout, ice, heads, showers, marine railway, launch ramp
Spanish POP 2AO	
Vance's Motor Inn, Box 190	Dining room
Chivilliiiihiil Dock	Launch ramp
Massey POP 1PO	
Blue Skies Motel, Box 642	Dining room
Mohawk Motel, Highway 17	
Pine Grove Motel, Box 637	Dining room, beach
Wayside Motel Friendship Inn, Box 717	
Espanola POP 1CO	
Avenue Hotel, Box 668	Dining room
Beltrami's Motel, Box 1730	
Clear Lake Inn, Box 194	Beach
Espanola Motor Hotel, Box 1156	
Goodman's Motel, Box 878	Dining room
Marshall's Espanola Motel, Box 932	Dining room
Pinewood Motor Inn, Box 1578	Dining room
Queensway Motel & Trailer Park, Box 1519	
Whitefish Falls POP 2HO	
Holiday Lodge	Dining room, boat rental, guides
	Gas, ice, water, electricity, showers, laundromat

Place by Post Office Address	Services
Government Dock	Launch ramp
Birch Island POP 1AO	
The Island Lodge	Dining room, beach, boat rental, guides
McGregor Bay	
Birch Island Lodge, Box 280	Dining room, boat rental, guides
Little Current POP 1KO	
Turner's McGregor Bay	Gas, ice
Frazer Bay	
Okeechobee Lodge, Box 850	Dining room, boat rental, guides
Little Current, POP 1CO	
	Dockage, gas, water, electricity, heads, showers, laundromat
Killarney POM 2AO	
Killarney Mountain Lodge	Dining room, cocktail lounge, outdoor pool, tennis, boat rental, guides
3 Commissioner Street	
	Dockage, gas, diesel, ice, electricity, water, pumpout, propane, heads, showers, launch ramp
Rock House Inn	Dining room, boat rental, guides
Channel Street	
Sportsman's Inn	Dining room, boat rental, guides
Channel Street	
	Dockage, gas, diesel, ice, water, electricity, pumpout, heads, showers, laundromat, launch ramp
A and R Marina	Gas, water, electricity, ice, head, shower
The George Islanders	Electricity, water, pumpout, heads, showers
Government Dock	Launch ramp

Place by Post Office Address	Services

Manitoulin Island

Evansville POP 1EO

Northernaire — Dining room, beach, boat rental, guides

Dockage, gas, water, electricity, ice, heads, showers, launch ramp

Gore Bay POP 1HO

Gordon's Lodge, Box 324 — Dining room, boat rental, guides, beach

Government Dock — Gas, diesel, water, ice, electricity, pumpout, heads, showers, launch ramp

Kagawong POP 1JO

Hideaway Lodge, Box 55 — Dining room, beach, boat rental

Government Dock — Gas, electricity, water, ice, pumpout, showers, launch ramp

Little Current POP 1KO

Anchor Inn, Box 670 — Dining room

Hawberry Motel, Box 123

Little Current Motel, Box 164

Sunset Motel, Box 488 — Boat rental, guides

Wagon Wheel Motel, Box 333

Government Dock — Gas, diesel, ice, pumpout, water, electricity, heads, showers, launch ramp

Little Current Marina — Gas, electricity, water, ice, pumpout, heads, showers

Manitowaning POP 1NO

Black Rock Resort, R.R.2 — Dining room, boat rental, beach

Hembruff's Motel, Box 75

Place by Post Office Address	Services
Lafleur Wayside Motel	Dining room
Manitowaning Lodge, Box 160	Dining room, outdoor pool, boat rental, launch ramp
Government Dock	Gas, diesel, pumpout, water, launch ramp
Meldrum Bay POP 1RO	
Meldrum Bay Inn	Dining room
Government Dock	Gas, diesel, water, ice, electricity, pumpout, heads, showers, launch ramp
Mindemoya POP 1SO	
Mindemoya Motel, R.R.1	Dining room
Timberland Lodge, R.R.1	Dining room, boat rental
Providence Bay POP 1TO	
Huron Sands Motel	Dining room
Government Dock	
Sheguiandah POP 1WO	
Red Lodge Resort, R.R.1	Dining room, boat rental, guides
Garrett's Roadside Motel	Dining room
Government Dock	
South Baymouth POP 1ZO	
Buck Horn Motel, Box 57	Coffee shop
Huron Motor Lodge, Box 10	
The Wigwam, Box 23	Dining room
Spring Bay POP 2BO	
Long Bay Lodge, R.R.3	Dining room, boat rental, beach
Rock Garden Terrace, R.R.1	Dining room, outdoor pool, sauna
West Bay (Excelsior)	
Government Dock	

Place by Post Office Address   Services

Wikwemikong
Government Dock

Yacht Charters

Blind River
Freedom Yacht Charters
Blind River Marina
P.O. Box 1644
Blind River, Ontario P0R 1B0

Gore Bay
Canadian Yacht Charters
243 College Street
Toronto, Ontario M5T 2Y1

Little Current
Discovery Yacht Charters
1732 Windle Drive
Sudbury, Ontario P3E 2Y5

Finncharters
R.R.1
Lively, Ontario P0M 2E0

Select Yacht Charters
2140 Regent Street
Sudbury, Ontario P3E 5S8

Appendix C

Marine Publications and How to Obtain Them

Order from: Hydrographic Chart Distribution Office
Department of Fisheries and Oceans
1675 Russell Road, P.O. Box 8080
Ottawa, Ontario K1G 3H6

Enclose check or money order payable in Canadian funds to Receiver General of Canada

	1987 Price
Catalogue of Nautical Charts and Related Publications	Free
Sailing Directions, Great Lakes, Volume II (latest edition)	$13.50
List of Lights, Buoys and Fog Signals, Inland Waters (published annually)	*N.A.*
Charts for the North Channel	$8.00 each

  2205—Killarney to Little Current
  2245—Beaverstone Bay to Lonely Island and McGregor Bay
  2250—Bruce Mines to Sugar Island
  2251—Meldrum Bay to St. Joseph Island
  2252—Clapperton Island to Meldrum Bay
  2257—Clapperton Island to John Island
  2258—Bayfield Sound and Approaches
  2259—John Island to Blind River
  2267—Great Duck Island to False Detour Passage
  2268—Plans in the North Channel
  2286—Georgian Bay to Clapperton Island
  2294—Little Current and Approaches

  Defoe Map available at Turner's, Little Current

Weekly "Notices to Mariners" with chart corrections are ordered from:
    Director, Aids and Waterways
    Canadian Coast Guard
    Ministry of Transport
    Ottawa, Ontario K1A ON7
Names are placed on the mailing list without charge.

Appendix D
More Reading About the North Channel

McQuarrie, W. John, editor-publisher, *Through The Years*, monthly publication dedicated to the recording of Manitoulin District history. Order from Mid-North Printers and Publishers, Ltd., P.O. Box 235, Gore Bay, Ontario, P0P 1H0. $2.95 per issue, plus $.65 postage and handling.

McDonald, J.E., *Yonder Our Island, One Hundred Years of History on Cockburn Island*, 1979. Order from the author at R.R.1, Thessalon, Ontario P0R 1L0

This is Manitoulin, Espanola, Tobermory and the North Channel. Obtainable at tourist information centers and at some stores in the region. Describes some localities and lists accommodations and services on Manitoulin Island and the east end of the north shore.

Canoe Routes of the North Georgian Bay Recreational Reserve, Ontario Ministry of Natural Resources, Whitney Block, 99 Wellesley Street West, Toronto, Ontario M7A 1W3.

Ontario Accommodations and *Ontario Camping*. Lists, by alphabetical place name, public accommodations and camping facilities, with post office addresses, number of accommodations, facilities and services offered. Available at all tourist information centers, or write Ontario Travel, Queen's Park, Toronto, Ontario M7A 2E5.

Inland Seas, quarterly journal of the Great Lakes Historical Society. Sometimes carries articles about North Channel history. Obtainable in libraries, or write to the Great Lakes Historical Society, 480 Main Street, Vermilion, Ohio 44089.

Local weekly newspapers, such as *The Manitoulin Expositor* and *The Gore Bay Recorder*, contain information about places of interest, planned events, and often publish special historical features.

Index

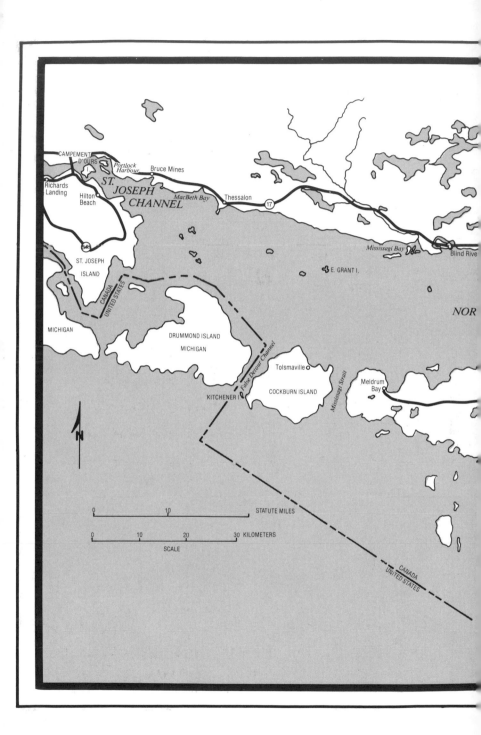